ONLINE MAREKTING DEVELOPMENT

JOHN LOK

ISBN 979-888591387-4

Contents

Foreword *v*

Prologue *vii*

1. Internet Technology Impacts Car And Publish And Housing Consumer Behaviors 1
2. Private Car Market Consumer Behavior 29
3. Publish Market Reader Behavior 47
4. Housing Market Buyer Behavior 77

Foreword

This book concerns to explain how and why private car and housing and publish markets which have different second hand car, house and book consumer behaviors. Global car and publishers and housing markest have similar consumer behavioral characteristcs. In car market, for example, car market has either new and old cars purchase or and rent cars service to let car consumers choices.

In private car market, car buyers can choose to buy any kinds of new or second hand cars from e-merchant car website stores or car shops easily. So, comparison any kinds of second hand cars prices or new cars prices or model and functions and designs is very easily from websites channel. Why technology , such as e-car merchant website store influences car buyers choice ?

In publish market, for example, publishers have ebooks or second hand paper books, even library lending service to let readers choose either visiting book shops to buy paper books or paying visa to read ebooks from online channel or visiting libraries to borrow books to read. Online and offline book shop competition is serious. Book readers have these both channel to choose to buy either electronic book or paper book to study. How can traditional offlince book shop achieve strategy to compete online book shop ? What are online book shop weaknesses or strengths? What are traditional offline book shop weaknesses or strengths? What is future book publishing development trend? These questions will have suggestions to be given to book publishers to let them to learn more marketing strategies.

So, house market, house buyers can choose to buy either second hand houses or new house from property shops or e-merchants website channel conveniently, also it means that competition is serious nowadays. Global houses demand may increase or decrease in any time. The month has many houses can sell easily, but it does not represent next month houses sale number can increase. What factors can influence house buyers‘ living need desires increase in long time? Why factors can influence house buyers' living need desires decrease in long time? How to apply behavioral economy thery in demand and supply view :demand (house buyer living demand) and supply (houses property developers sale number) to evaluate whether the year has how many house buyers hope to buy houses to live in the country's house market. Global houses demand may increase or decrease in any time. The month has many houses can sell easily, but it does not represent next month houses sale number can increase. What factors can influence house buyers‘ living need desires increase in long time? Why factors can influence house buyers’ living need desires decrease in long time?

In house market discussion, I shall indicate US and UK developed countries how property sellers website stores influence UK and US house buyers‘ second hand house and new house choice. I shall explain how applying economy theories solve economic problems, why does economic environment can have indirect influence to property buyers’ property purchase desire. I shall explain how to apply behavioral economic method to predict house buyers purchase living desire. I shall explain how to predict property market development in property market demand and supply view as well as what the main factors influence future US and UK second hand and new house buyer choices when the US and UK property sellers apply their e-stores to let any internet users to find their second hand and new hand house photos from internet. This property chapter concerns to explain how UK and US property developers apply internet to influence US and UK second hand and new houses choices.

I shall give reasons and evidences to support my idea. In behavioral economy view, I shall explain how internet influence shouse , book buyers and private car buyers their demand desires in global new or second hand housing , publishing and private car market why these markets consumers as well as how their second hand book, house and car consumer behavior and ecommerce sale methods are different.

Prologue

Table of content

Chapter 1

Internet Technology Impacts Car And Publish And Housing Consumer Behaviors

● Demand And Supply Theory Solves Consumer Problems Examples p.5-30

● Demand and supply view to housing , publish and private car markets

● Basic income level influences car and book and housing buyer either purchase second hand book or used car or second hand house or rent house borrow book or rent car or purchase new book or new car or new house decision

Chapter 2

Private Car Market Consumer Behavior

● Why does technological factor raise rental car service need p.31-50

● Car past driving safe record report performance influences car buyer choice

● The car buyer or car renter making decision process

● Non price factor influences automobiles buyers' needs or desires

Demand view to influence car buyer demand

1.Weather factor influences car buyer demand

2.The price of substitutes factor influences car buyer demand

3.The complementary goods to automobiles factor influence car buyer demand

4.The income distribution factor influence car buyer demand

5.Future expectations factor influences car buyer demand

Supply view to influence car buyer demand
1.Production costs factor influences car buyer demand
2.The profitability of alternatives factor influences car buyer demand
3.The aims of the car producers factor influences car buyer demand
4. The unpredictable events or nature acts factor influences car buyer demand

- Factors that determine the price elasticity of supply of automobiles
- What's the effect of the used car market on car price and seond hand book price similar consumer behavioral characteristics?
- Technology influences the car user demand change for the Auto Industry

Chapter 3
Publish Market Reader Behavior
- Library Services in the Digital Age p.51-68
- Public priorities for libraries
- Changes in library use in recent years
- How people use libraries
- Second hand book market
- Is It Best to Buy or Borrow Books?

Online vs offline book shop different devlopment trend
- Pricing strategy in online and offline book retailing p.69-74
- Web vs School campus book store development trend

Prediction of direction of electronic books future trend
- What are the factors to influence sales and marketing strategies for publishers?

Analysis of factors influencing online newspaper reading behavior
p.75-85

● How electronic versus traditional print textbook influence of university students' learning behavior

● How to change future e-reader study habit to feel better

● Factors influence child reading habit

Chapter 4

Housing Market Buyer Behavior

Internet impacts second hand and new house buyers purchase living desire

● Property market demand and supply view p.86-118

US and UK property market development

● Low mortgage rates will help US homebuyers afford property

1. US property geographic building location choice factor
2. High property material production cost and labor hortage factor can influence property price rises in US property market
3. Long time low renting property to live factor

● What Drives US and UK Property Market Supply and Demand

● Property supply and demand is driven by both local and general factors.

● Prediction property market trend within one to two year in demand and supply theory analysis

● What are the main factors influence the future England and America property market future development

CHAPTER ONE

Internet Technology Impacts Car And Publish And Housing Consumer Behaviors

- Demand And Supply Theory Solves Consumer Problems Examples

What is economy rule predict consumer behaviour? Why and How does economist can apply economy rule to predict consumer behaviours? I shall explain the reasons as below:

Why does economic principle be the best to predict consumer behaviour. It may include these two reasons: The first focuses on the substantive domain of study, in this interpretation , economics is a social science devoted to understanding how the economy works. The second definition focuses on methods: economics is a way of doing social science, using particular tools. In this interpretation the discipline is associated with formal modelling and statistical analysis rather than particular hypotheses or theories about the economy. Therefore, economic methods can be applied to many other areas besides the economy, everything from decisions within the family to questions about political institutions.

- Demand and supply principle predict public transport tool passenger behaviour

Economists need to use the right economic ideas to predict consumer behaviour. So, Misuse the wrong economy ideas to predict consumer behaviours. It will do more wrong judgement to evaluate or predict why and how and when the country's consumer behaviours will change. It is every economist needs to consider issue. For example, the economy idea application of economic supply-demand principles to public transport. Different fares would give commuters with more-flexible hours the incentive to avoid peak travel times. They would allow passenger traffic to spread out over time, reducing the pressure on the public transport system when enabling even larger total passenger flow. IT aims to reduce traffic congestion, increased public-transport use, reduced car-bon emissions and cause air pollution and generated considerable revenue for the country's transport system. So, if the country can apply supply and demand economic principle to attempt to predict how many passengers number needs to catch transport tools to go to work or go to school or other activities. Then, it can predict how many bus, ferry, taxi, train, underground train, tram etc. different public transport tools to satisfy future public transport passengers' needs in society. So, this demand and supply principle is the comparative best rule to predict any kinds of public transport passengers' road needs, when they need to either go to school, go to office, go to leisure or shopping etc. different kinds of activities. So, applying the demand and supply principle to predict road and sea public transport passengers can help the country to reduce air pollution when they feel that they can find any public transport tools to catch any time conveniently , then it can encourage them to reduce car purchase desire. When many people choose to catch public transport tools, then it will reduce many cars number on the road. Then, air pollution will reduce as well as any public transport tools' income will also increase as well as traffic jam will also reduce. When the country can evaluate how many people choose to catch bus or taxi or ferry or train or underground train, or tram or train etc. different kinds of public transport tools, then the country can predict the more accurate public transport tools number to every kind of public transport tool to satisfy their journey needs. e.g. whether underground train or train or tram need to decrease or increase the frequent times or number to catch the volume of passenger in busy or non-busy time; or whether bus company has need to increase how much buses to catch the city location passengers when they are living in the city. Moreover, supply and demand principle can help any public transport tools to explain why their passengers number reduces in the year, it may due to fare charge is unreasonable, feeling uncomfortable to sit on the seat or air condition is poor in the transport tool environment, or there are no more seats because many there are much time is full passenger and no seat vacancy to provide to them to sit .

So, supply and demand principle can help any kinds of public transport tools to find whether which is (are) the factor(S) can influence the current or last year passengers number reduce. Then, they can concentrate on improving their weaknesses to raise their service quality . So, supply and demand principle can also help they to evaluate whether what their weakness are in order to improve to increase passengers number. They can do questionnaires to enquiry their passengers' response to evaluate whether which areas of services that they feel unsatisfactory. So, the different kinds of service satisfactory feeling to the passengers number data will be the main source to help the kind of public transport tool to analyse and conclude the results more accurate, then they can make the more accurate judgement to improve the of service. For example, the questionnaires indicate that the many passengers feel the bus fare is reasonable, but many passengers feel they can not find any seats to sit easily. So, it implies that the bus firm ought buy more buses or enlarges bus size and increases more seats in the enlarged buses. Then, it does not reduce its fare but it needs to find solutions to let passengers can find seats to sit in every bus more easily. But, if the questionnaires indicate that there are many passengers feel its fare is higher or unreasonable to compare other kinds of public transportation tools. Hence, it can avoid to spend more expenditure to increase bus number to the city, if the city has many passengers , they still choose bus to catch, but they feel its fare is too higher to compare other kinds of public transport tool. Then, it only needs to reduce its fare , it ought help it to increase passengers number. Hence, demand and supply principle is the most suitable economic method to evaluate any kinds of public transport system passenger needs in any country nowadays.

- How to supply consumer choice theory to predict Consumer Behavior Marketing at Apple Computer

During US economy growth, Apply computer applies consumer choice theory to solve its computer buyers' choice problems among different kinds of brand computer competitors. Have you ever wondered why Apple is so successful? They were not the first company to invent the personal computer, portable music device, the tablet, the smartphone, software to download music, or the set-top box to name a few. Apple has amassed a brand loyal following like no other brand backed by significant sales, market share, and profitability. So, how does Apple do it? What's the secret behind their success?

Marketing using consumer behavior insight is how Apple succeeds. Even though Steve Jobs and Apple, did not use consumer research in the initial development of most products, consumer behavior plays a huge role in their marketing and ultimately the success of the company. Once a consumer purchases a product or downloads iTunes Apple has access to data the company leverages. Apple uses this information to gain significant insight into the consumer and what drives purchase behavior.

Consumer behavior marketing is an essential ingredient in the current business climate. The companies that apply this type of marketing well have a distinct competitive advantage that distances them from their rivals. Consumer behavior research is the primary driver at the core of any good strategy. Research provides actionable insight and ensures business success. If you answer no to the following questions, this post is for you?

•Are you applying consumer behavior marketing currently?

•Have you conducted consumer behavior research within the last two years?

•Do you have consumer behavior marketing in your marketing plan with well-defined marketing strategies and tactics?

•Are you achieving the maximum results for your organization?

Every business has a target audience and consumer behavior marketing provides the fundamental methods for understanding your target. Consumer behavior research provides the underlying element that drives quality strategies and ensures business results.

"Marketing is understanding your buyers really, really well. Then creating valuable products, services, and information especially for them to help solve their problems."

The organizations that have an intimate understanding of their target audience possess a competitive advantage over those that do not. Establishing a one-to-one relationship and thorough knowledge of your target audience is a core responsibility for business in the 21st century and beyond. Regardless if you are B2B, B2C, B2G or a hybrid organization you have a target audience. The information in this post can be applied to any business type. This post focuses on Apple (B2C) employing consumer behavior marketing as a critical ingredient for their success.

Hence, Apply computer shops have several computer teachers to teach any visitors how to use its laptops, hen they enquire its any computer salespeople. Due to its salespeople had been trained to learn how to use the different kinds of laptops. So, anyone enquires them, they can answer their enquires concern any computer questions immediately. Then, they will feel Apple laptops are the first choice to compare other kinds of laptops brands. It is one salespeople answering strategies to persuade any Apple computer visitors to feel its any laptops are the first or preference choice to compare its competitors in this computer market, so customer choice economic theory is the most suitable strategy to solve Apple computer's customer individual purchase decision problem.

Economists such as Carl Menger, William Stanley Jevons and Marie-Esprit-Léon Walras. and Alfred Marshall developed ideas such as diminishing marginal utility. Many of these neo-classical economic theories were brought together in Alfred Marshall's very influential textbook, Principles of Economics. (1890)

•Note there is some blurring between classical economics and neo-classical economics.

•Neo-classical economics has also come to mean 'orthodox economic theory. To a large extent, it has incorporated new developments in microeconomics, such as theories of market failure, market structure and econometrics.

Theories of Market failure

Neo-classical economics has become associated with a belief in the efficiency of markets. However, microeconomic theory has also incorporated the criticisms and limitations of free-markets.

•Monopoly. Adam Smith was well aware of the problem of monopolies and how firms could use their market power to set excessive prices.

•Imperfect competition. In the 1930s, Joan Robinson developed a model of imperfect competition, an awareness many markets were somewhere between monopoly and perfect competition often assumed in neo-classical economics.

•Externalities. Developed by Arthur C.Pigou in The Economics of Welfare (1920) this is the awareness production and consumption decisions can have harmful (or positive) effects on third parties. Therefore, a free market can lead to overconsumption of demerit goods and negative externalities.

•Game theory. An awareness, decisions are not linear or simple, but the interdependence of agents influences what we decide to do.

Behavioural economics

The most important trend in recent decades in economics is the greater emphasis placed on aspects of behavioural economics, which uses many insights from related fields such as psychology.

•Disputes rational choice theory. The essential element of behavioural economics is that it argues individual agents are often not rational and often do not seek to maximise utility.

•Behavioural economics examines how agents can be influenced by biases, and make decisions not predicted by neo-classical economic theory. Behavioural economics can explain the irrational exuberance of booms and busts.

Econometrics

In the post-war period, economics became increasingly mathematical with economists attempting to use mathematics to explain models and theories. Econometrics looks at economic data and seeks to extract simple relationships. The basic tool is the linear regression models and can be used to try and predict consumer spending and demand for labour.

Heterodox models of microeconomics

Heterodox models differ substantially from microeconomic foundations of neo-classical economics. Schools of thought include

Marxist economic theory

Karl Marx developed an alternative perspective on economics. He focused on the surplus value created under the capitalist economic system. To Marx, the invisible hand of the market would be better described as the invisible hand of capitalist exploitation of workers. Marx claimed workers did receive their full labour value but were compensated for their necessary labour only – enabling capitalists to profit from the surplus.

Institutional economics. The role of society and institutions in shaping economic behaviour. For example, Thomas Veblen looked at theories of 'conspicuous consumption' and noted how the desire for social status could drive much economic theory. Institutional economics could be seen as a forerunner for later behavioural economics.

Environmental economics Argues traditional economics wrongly places value on increasing output. The most important thing is creating a sustainable environment which maximises living standards. So, manufacturers need to consider how to manufacture their products , but pollution can not be raised as the same time, because human will face to raise cost of living and living experiences to be poor , even food shortage, water pollution , air pollution , death rate raises when technological productivities brings pollution to our natural environment. Hence, environmental economoic theory is the most suitable to solve manufacturers' pollution problem.

Buddhist economics/non-profit goals. Like environmental economics, this questions the assumption higher incomes and higher output are desirable.

The theory of hedonistic relativism suggests higher incomes do nothing to increase happiness levels, and traditional economics can encourage society to pursue materialistic goals which actually create more problems of stress, conflict and environmental degradation.

Some of the basic models you might find in A-Level economics :

•Price Discrimination

•Perfect competition

•Price Mechanism

•Monopoly

•Oligopoly and kinked demand curve

•Game Theory Pricing strategies

•Market failure

•Behavioural economics

ON conclusion, any macro economy theories can be applied to find the most reasonable methods to solve any customer problems in societies by economists as above. So, I believe that any economic and customer and social problems can be solved by economic theories in our society.

● Demand and supply view to housing , publish and private car markets

The consumer problem – sometimes called the basic or central consumer emotion or psychological problem – asserts that an industry or market, such as these two car rent or purchase market and ebook or paper book purchase or rent market. These two market have infinite resources are insufficient to satisfy all human wants and needs. Why does book market or car market will have insufficient infinite books or card resources to satisfy car consumers' driving entetainment need or readers' reading need ?

For the shop market example, the reader can not find whose interesting books to buy from the book shop or library. Then he will choose the another book shop or library to find whose interesting reading of book. Even, if the book shop or library can not provide his interesting book to buy or borrow. Then, the reader will continue to go to next book shop or library to continue research the book, till to he can find the interesting reading book to buy or borrow from library or book shop. I suppose that the reader is one student , he must need to find the book to finish his assignment for his reference. So, in this moment, the kind of topic book may be shortage to supply to let the reader, e.g. student to buy or borrow at the moment, it may be due to many readers had borrowed the kind of topic books (the publisher's book) from any libraries or many readers had purchased the kind of topic books (the publisher's book) from any book shops. So, in this book market, it is possible to cause the kind of topic book from the publisher , it is shortage when the number of readers choice to purchase the topic of the book , this topic book's readers' demand number is more than the publishing number or printing sale number to the book (supply number). So, the book's price must increase when the readers number is more than it's publishing sale number in the short time. For the car market example, when the car manufacture can sell the kind of new style car to attract many car buyers to choose to buy to drive, but the car manufacturers has limited supply number to the new kind of style car to sell in the market. So, the new kind of style car price may increase because its car buyers number is more than its supply number in the short time. So, in car and book market, their supply may be shortage , because the car manufacturers or publishers control to print the limited number books to publish or manufacture the limited number cars to sell, when they feel there are many readers like to read the topic of identified author's book or they feel there are many car buyers like to drive the indentified style of car. Then, they will avoid to publish the author's book number is more than reader number or avoid to manufacture the kind of style car number is more than the kind of style car buyer number. So, when the kind of car production is reduced or the author's book publishing number is reduced, but the author's readers number is increasing or the style of car buyers number is increasing. Then, although the publisher or the car seller can increase their price , but their reader number to the author's book , it won't decrease or their style car number to the car buyers , it won't decrease, because demand is more than supply. It is any kind of style car product and any author their demand and supply similar characteristics. Economics involves the study of how to allocate resources in conditions of scarcity However, viewing economics as the study of how society allocates resources can lead to conflation of normative economic planning and empirical study of how economic agents operate in these conditions. So, economic demand and supply view can be applied to explain why some authors' book price or some kind of style new car price can be increased seriously, but their buyers number will not decrease in the short time.

In mainstream neoclassical economics, it is assumed that humans pursue their self-interest, and that the market mechanism best satisfies the various wants different individuals might have. These wants are often divided into individual wants (which depend on the individual's preferences and purchasing power parity) and collective wants (which are the wants of entire groups of people). Things such as food and clothing can be classified as either wants or needs, depending on what type and how often a good is requested. So, such as book market case, because any readers must pursue to find the most attractive or interesting book content's book to them to choose to read among different similar topic books as well as such as car market case, any car buyers must pursue to choose the most cheapest and the most safe and the more enjoyable feeling and the most more function style car to buy among different similar styles of cars. So, in neoclassical economics demand and supply theory, it can explain why readers and car buyers will need more time to choose to buy any topic of books or any styles of cars because they do not want to choose the under value of book to read or under value of car to drive if they do not visit more book shops or libraries or car shops to compare their similar styles of cars or similar author's topic books in order to make the accurate shopping decision.

However, economists have sometimes characterized "how" to produce as a "technological problem" of efficiency whereas the allocation of what is produced is an "economic problem". In a free market, the "how" of production and allocation of resources is distributed among economic agents. In a centrally planned economy, a principal decides how and what to produce on behalf of agents. Modern economies are often welfare capitalist with various regulations, which makes the economic system more equitable while retaining the distributed free market system. Due to human wants are unlimited, an infinite series of human wants remains continue with human life. Nobody can claim that all of his wants have been satisfied and he has no need to satisfy any further want. Everybody feels hunger at a time then other he needs water. Sometime one feels the desire of clothing then starts to feel the desire of having good conveyance. When all existing wants are satisfied then new wants starts to create in mind, so the series of wants remains continue till the last moment of life. So an economic problem arises because of existence of unlimited human wants. It means that choice problem to any car buyer or book buyer arises because of existence of unlimited interesting learning needs to any readers or unlimited driving enjoyable needs to any car buyers.

● The problem of full employment of resources to publishing and car markets

In view of how to use available labour resources are fully utilized is an important one factor to influence car seller and book publishing in success.

A community should achieve maximum satisfaction by using the scarce resources in the best possible manner—not wasting resources or using them inefficiently. There are two types of employment of resources:

(1) Labour-intensive to publishers and car manufacturers

In capitalist economies, however, available labbour resources are not fully used, such as car designer or technician (skilled labour) as well as creative author (creative writting labour) in this car and publish business environment. In times of depression, many people want to work but can't find employment, such as there are many people are unemploying or lose jobs, so their car purchase desires will decrease . So, many car designers or car manufacturing technicians will lose jobs in car industry. But, in times of depression, otherwise, publish industry will have more sale chance because many people lose jobs, then they will spend more time to visit book shops to find interesting books to buy to read. It supposes that the scarce resources are not fully utilized in a capitalistic economy. So, such as publishers must need to find enough number authors to let them to help them to create any new topic books to satisfy their readers' different reading needs. Hence, author (creative labour) is one main factor to influence the publisher's book sale number. If the publisher has many creactive authors , they like to give themselves written books to let it to help them to publish, then the creative authors can help the publisher to increase readers or book buyers number , even its book prices to the author will not decrease in order to attract many readers. So, creative authors (written labours) factor is more important to influence any publishers' books sale number. So, such as car manufacturers must need to find enough car technicians to help them to design any new and more unique function cars to attract any car buyers to choose to buy. So, car technicians or designer (labor) will also be one important factor to influence their car sale number.

● The problem of economic growth

If productive capacity grows, an economy can produce progressively more goods, which raises the standard of living. Such as car market. When many people have jobs, they have enough money to buy cars to drive in order to satisfy their driving leisure feel. The increase in productive capacity of an economy is called economic growth. There are various factors affecting economic growth. The problems of economic growth have been discussed by numerous growth models, including the Harrod-Domar model, the neoclassical growth models of Solow and Swan, and the Cambridge growth models of Kaldor and Joan Robinson. This part of the economic problem is studied in the economies of development.

● Needs and wants problems (economic growth or economic recession) to influence car or book buyers' consumption desires.

Needs are things or material items of peoples need for survival, such as food, clothing, housing, and water. Everyone has a different needs and wants. Until the Industrial Revolution, the vast majority of the world's population struggled for access to basic human needs.

Wants are effective desires for a particular product, or for something that can only be obtained by working for it. While the fundamental needs of survival are key in the function of the economy, wants are the driving force that stimulates demand for goods and services. To curb the economic problem, economists must classify the nature and different wants of consumers, as well as prioritize wants and organize production to satisfy as many wants as possible. So, when economic growth, many people have jobs to work, any cheap cars can be sold to low income level car buyers very easily, even, expensive cars , many high income level people will choose higher price cars to buy to drive. However, one country has real economic problem, it depends on whether how long time people can have stable jobs to work in societies. It implies that economic growth factor can influence car buyers number to increase. Otherwise, economic growth factor can influence book buyers number to decrease, but many people need work, they won't have more time to visit book shops. Because visiting book shops times are decreasing to any one when they need to work, then their purchase book chance will also decrease.

● Five bases problems of demand and supply to publisher and car seller

In our book reading and car driving societies , in general, our societies will have these similar problems to our book and car sale markets. The following points highlight the five basic problems of an economy to influence publishing and car sale market succeed. The problems are:

1. Car manufacturing industry economic problem:

a. Choice which style of design cars to produce when car maufacturing materials are limited to supply and in what quantities to manufacture the kind of style of car ?

a. How to use the limited materials to produce the different kinds of style cars.

c. The kind style of cars are produced for whom more in order to decide which style of cars are produced in preference, when there are same number of car buyers choose to buy the two kinds or more of style or cars in the same time, but time is not enough and manufacturing materials are not enough to be supplied to let these styles or cars can be produced to supply in the same time. (How Efficiently are the Resources being utilized?)

2. Publishing industry book sale problem:

Is the Economy Growing? Choice whom author(s) books to publish, when the book shop has not enough warehouse to keep all authors' book in store and in what quantities to print for ever author's books. Because when economy is growing, there are many people have jobs to do, so they won't spend more time to visit book shops. Then, book shop needs to choose the most attractive authors‘ books to put on themselves shelves in order to persuade them to make book purchase decision because they won't spend more time to stay in book shop, e.g. working lunch hours or working office hours. They will feel that they need more time to go to sleep when they feel tried after working time.

Problem 1:What to Produce and in What Quantities to car manufacturing industry

The first central problem of an economy is to decide what goods and services are to be produced and in what quantities in car manufacturing industry, e.g. which kinds of styles cars and what quantities of different kinds of styles car manufacturing. This involves allocation of scarce resources (car manufacturing materials) in relation to the composition of total output in the economy. Since resources (car manufacturing materials component) are scarce, the car manufacturers have to decide about which kinds of styles design cars to be manufacture in preference. Once the nature of the kinds of styles cars choicen to be produced is decided, then their quantities are to be decided. Since the resources (car manufacturing material, e.g. steel, equipment, motor, wheel) of the economy are scarce, the problem of the nature of car styles of manufacturing choices and their quantities has to be decided on the basis of priorities or preferences of the society.

If the society gives priority to the production of more consumer goods, e.g. television , computer , waching machine they need more steel material to be manufactured now, it will have less in the future. A higher priority on capital goods , such as car implies less consumer goods now and more in the future. But since steel material resources are scarce, if some goods are produced in larger quantities, such as cars , some other goods will have to be produced in smaller quantities, such as computer . Suppose the economy produces capital goods and consumer goods. In deciding the total output of the economy, the society has to choose that combination of capital goods and consumer goods which is in keeping with its resources. So, in the year, if the country has many consumers need to buy computers, washing machines etc. consumer products which are needed to use more steel material to manufacture, then the country will have less steel materials to be supplied to car manufacturers to use to manufacture cars , due to the steel manufacturing material has shortage to supply problem to the car manufacturers because many consumer products are used to produce computers, washinc machines etc. products in the year.

Problem 2: How to Produce these Goods, such as different kinds of design styles of cars

The next basic problem of an economy is to decide about the techniques or methods (e.g. robotic machines are used to manufacture cars or traditional manual to be used in order to produce the required goods, such as different kinds of design styles of cars. This problem is primarily dependent upon the availability of resources, such as how many robotic machines and manual manufacturing workers , the car manufacturing firm owns . If factory area is large available in abundance, it may have robotic and manual both or robotic replaces human worker to manufacture cars in the large factory. If factory area is scarce, intensive methods of all robotic are not suitable because robotic size is also large. So, manual car manufacturing workers may be more suitable used. If labour is in abundance, it may use labour- intensive techniques to manufacure cars; while in the case of labour shortage, capital-intensive, such as robotic car manufacturing techniques may be used.

The technique to be used also depends upon the type and quantity of goods to be produced. For producing capital goods, such as cars and large outputs, complicated and expensive machines and techniques , such as robotics are required. On the other hand, simple consumer goods, such as computer and small outputs require small and less expensive machines and comparatively simple techniques.

Problem 3. For whom is the Goods Produced , such as expensive cars or cheap cars?

The third basic problem to be decided is the allocation of goods among the members of the society. The allocation of basic consumer goods or necessities and luxuries comforts and among the household takes place on the basis of among the distribution of national incom, such as manufacturing how many expensive cars and how many cheap cars. Whosoever possesses the means to buy the goods may have then. A rich person may have a large share of the luxuries goods, such as expensive cars and a poor person may have more quantities of the basic consumer goods he needs, such as cheap cars. Hence, car manufacturers need to predict how many rich people and poor people or high income and low income people, they are living in the country in order to evaluate whether how many expensive cars and how many cheap cars to be manufacture in the year.

Problem 4: How Efficiently are the Resources being Utilised to car manufacture?

This is one of the important basic problems of an economy because having made the three earlier decisions, the society has to see whether the resources it owns are being utilized fully or not. In case the resources of the economy are lying idle, it has to find out ways and means to utilize them fully. Such as car manufacturers, every car manufacturer needs to predict whether their different kinds of style design cars need to be utilized to spend how many steel material etc. resources to manufacture when the country or society has many consumers need to buy the cheap consumption products, such as computer, televison which are needed to use steel materials to produce because steel material will have shortage to supply problem to the country's car manufacturers in the year.

Problem 5: Is the Economy Growing benefits to car manufacture?

The last and the most important problem is to find out whether the economy is growing through time or is it stagnant. If the economy is stagnant at any point inside the production possibility curve, it has to be moved on to the production possibility curve PP whereby the economy now produces larger quantities of consumer goods and capital goods. Economic growth takes place through a higher rate of capital formation which consists of replacing existing capital goods with new and more productive ones by adopting more efficient production techniques or through innovations. So, such as car manufaturing industry, if the country is economy growing, many people will have more jobs to work and they have more money to buy cars to drive. Then, robotic car manufacturing techniques will be more suitable to car manufacturing industry because there are many cars needs will increase in short time in the year.

All of these economy problems will be any countries' car manufacturers often cause feel need to solve resource shortage problems in order to achieve enough steel or other car manufacturing material resources to manufacture the enough number of different kinds of style design cars to let any one kind of style design car buyer can buy in any time.

● The Consumer Problem in car and publish markets

Consumer theory is concerned with how a rational consumer would make consumption decisions. What makes this problem worthy of separate study, apart from the general problem of choice theory, is its particular structure that allows us to derive economically meaningful results. The structure arises because the consumer's choice sets are assumed to be defined by certain prices and the consumer's income or wealth. The consumer's problem is to choose that is most preferred or, equivalently, that has the greatest utility.

The assumption of perfect information is built deeply into the formulation of this choice problem, just as it is in the underlying choice theory, such as which topic book or whom author will be readers' preference of book purchase choice in book publishing market as well as which kind of style design car will be car buyers' preference of car purchase choice in car sale market.

Some alternative models treat the consumer as rational but uncertain about the products, for example how a particular book brings the reader feel interest to read or a how well a car will perform to satisfy the car buyer's need. Some goods may be experience goods which the consumer can best learn about by trying ("experiencing") the good, such as car. In that case, the consumer might want to buy some now and decide later whether to buy more. That situation would need a different formulation. Similarly, if the agent thinks that high price goods, such as expensive cars are more likely to perform in a satisfactory way, that, too, would suggest quite a different formulation to compare cheap cars. Agents (car sellers) are price-takers. The agent takes prices p as known, fixed and exogenous. This assumption excludes things like searching for better prices or bargaining for a discount of car.

Hence , it seems that (whether the year's economy is growing or recessing) economic problems and consumer problems (whether the consumer have more time to choose or high or low consumption desire)are similar, I feel that it is possible , economists can attempt to apply any economic theories to solve some consumer problems in some situations. They can find the accurate solutions when they can apply the suitable economic theories to solve the suitable consumer or economic problems in our societies, such as car and book market cases. I shall indicate that how economists can apply the suitable economic theories to attempt to solve some consumer problems in our societies as below:

Demand And Supply Theory Solves Consumer Problems in car and book markets

● What Is Market Analysis – Demand and Supply?

In the field of business, it is important for establishments and corporations, such as publishing firms or car manufacturing firms to ensure that they take corporate decisions that can positively affect the business and its operations. This is the reason why market analysis is an essential process that should be taken seriously by any management. Market analysis is not only centered in identifying the correct prospective markets but also in specifically knowing the demands of various market niches and how these demands can affect the supply of the business.

● Supply Inventory Examples & Samples, such as the cars are displayed on the car shops and the books are displayed on the book shops

As a concept of economics, the study on supply and demand can help businesses become more effective and efficient when it comes to knowing the condition of the market, the current needs and wants of current and prospective customers, and how the business should react on varying circumstances. Having a marketing analysis elements with regards demand and supply can contribute to the growth and development of the business. So, some styles of cars displayed or some authors of books displayed which can help the car or book sellers to evaluate whether whom authors' books are more popular to be sold to any readers or which kinds of styles of cars are more popular to be sold to any car buyers when they are displayed to let any readers or car buyers to observate ad enquire salespeople any opinions about the book content or the car function, then they will make puchase decisions when they compare their choices. Consequently , car sellers or book sellers can know whether whom authors' books are more popular or which kinds of style design cars are more popular.

● Importance of Including Demand and Supply Review in Market Analysis to car and book publish markets

Customers are important to be studied so that businesses can ensure that they cater to both the needs and wants of the market. The activities of people can greatly affect the operation and production of companies which is why market analysis is commonly focused on knowing the movement of a particular market niche. It is important to include a demand and supply review within a market analysis example for the following reasons:

1. The pricing of goods and products, such as the displayed higher price or low price books, displayed expensive or cheap cars can actually be affected by the market demand. Supplying the appropriate price for products in a timely manner can make the business more trustworthy and credible.

2. If businesses will be aware of the demand for a product, then they can do measures to either maintain or improve their production. This can also be helpful if there is a need to decrease product quantity especially if the market does not respond to a specific product well, such as expensive or cheap displayed cars as well as higher or lower book price

3. Having an initial demand and supply review can help companies easily identify the factors that can affect the purchasing or acquisition power of customers. This will lead to the development of answers with regards to what the market currently needs.

● The Formation of Market Equilibrium through Demand and Supply to car market

Car Companies need to find a balance between their production and operations. A market analysis helps a lot in giving the market equilibrium that can help the business a lot. Forming market equilibrium or the appropriate and timely intersection of the demand curve and supply curve can give the business goals more possibilities for higher revenue and lesser production expenses. Here is why market equilibrium is important:

1. If the car products produced by a car firm checklist is just enough to supply the demands of its customers, then shortages or overproduction can be minimized. This can help the business allocate the right amount of money for car products that will surely not go to waste either due to expiration or unsuitability to the needs of the market resulting in loss of sales.

2. Changes in the car price of products and/or salepeople services can be well guided if a study of the car market demand and supply is already present. This is beneficial both to car customers and the car sale business as they can easily understand the price movement of certain items.

3. Reducing car supply in a measured time frame can give businesses the advantage of focusing its financial goals and efforts on developing new products that will sell. If the demand is not that high anymore and the business is aware of it, then proper metrics of operations can be implemented.

● Factors to Consider when Analyzing Demand and Supply to book and car both markets

If the book shop or car seller analysis to build a market research plan is guided by the elements of macroeconomics, then it is for sure that both graphic representation and discussion of demand and supply curves are presented accordingly. There are several factors that are necessary to be considered for a demand and supply analysis to be correctly implemented. Some of the determinants that the book shop or car seller needs to be knowledgeable of are listed below.

1. Demand determinants are external factors that can directly impact the activities of customers. Demand determinants are important to be reviewed as businesses need to be aware of how their market can potentially welcome the book or car product in the marketplace. Demand determinants are as follows:

1. The current social status of the reading or car drivig market
2. The income bracket where the current and potential market of the business belongs, such as whether how many public libraries can borrow the author's books to read or how many book shops can sell the author's books, or whether how many car shops can sell the similar styles of design cars
3. The product preferences of the market especially in relation to price points, e.g. whether the similar topic of authors' books prices are lower or higher or whether the similar kinds of styles design cars prices are lower or higher
4. The current expectations of the market for car products or topic of book of the same kind
5. The range of customers that can potentially benefit from the car product or book and/or salespeople service offers
6. The taste of the customers in relation to car design, book contents and/or salespeople service quality, customer care and the like

2. Supply determinants are the items that can affect the production of the company's supplies. The most important factors that you have to be

aware of when determining the appropriate amount of supply include the following:

1. The review of the expected car product or the author 's book prices in the future
2. The capital or cost of production that the car company or book publish will shoulder
3. The finances of the car or book company and how a particular car similar design or book similar content can affect it
4. The labor or manpower that the business needs to employ and pay to achieve car production effectively
5. The completion and full existence of all the materials, items and technology for the car production, e.g. robotic

In car manufacturing or book publish industries, if your market research and analysis contains information about the demand and supply curve, then it will be faster for you to execute actions with regards to your production schedule and overall operations. Your relationship with your market matters the most which are why you need to know what they need in varying time periods.

As specified, supply and demand analysis can affect book or car pricing and car production or book printing in general. Being knowledgeable of specific details especially those listed above can positively affect the company and how it is perceived by the marketplace. Demand and supply analysis, as well as the entire market analysis, should be updated from time to time so that the management agenda can make sure that they are aware of the current market trends and activities. Make the most out of having a demand and supply study in your market analysis and see how it can affect your business in a positive manner. What is economy rule predict consumer behaviour in car or book markets? Why and How does economist can apply economy rule to predict consumer behaviours in car or book markets? I shall explain the reasons as below:

- Rationing by book or car or housing prices

By determining the equilibrium prices and quantities of all inputs and outputs, the market allocated or rations out the scare goods of the society among the possible uses. Who does the rationing? A planning board? Congress or the president? BO, the marketplace, through the interaction of supply and demand, doe the rationing. This is rationing by the purse.

What cars are produced or whom author's books are published or what house design has more need? This is answered by the signals of the market price. High oil prices stimulates oil production, whereas low food prices drive resources out of agriculture. Those who have the most dollars votes have the greatest influences on what goods are produced. All of these considers how demand and supply to the market.

For whom are goods produces? The power of the pursue indicates the distribution of income and consumption. Those with higher incomes end up with expensive cars needs

Even, the how question is decided by supply and demand. When corn prices are low, it is not profitable for farmers to use expensive tractors and irrigation systems, and only the best land is cultivated. When oil prices are high, oil companies drill in deep offshore waters and employ novel seismic techniques to find oil. So, car and book prices are same to follow farmer and oil manufactuers' prices decision method.

IN sum , any thing needs through demands, interact with costs of goods, as reflected in supplies in our economic world. Hence, demand and supply theory ought be the most accurate method to help any businesses or governments to predict their shareholders behaviours when they will change as well as how and why their behaviours change , e.g. why the author's books sale number is less or increase or why the style of design car sale number is less or increase or why the kind of house design sale number is less or increase. The rational price factor will have some relationship to influence their sale number , but it is not the main factor to influence their sale number changes.

● Basic income level influences car and book buyer and housing buyer either purchase second hand book or used car or send hand house or borrow book or rent car or rent house or purchase new book or new car or new house individual spending behavioral choice

Can apply behavioral economic method to predict that the consequences of a stable basic income level how to influence housing, private car and book consumer's consumption behavior? However, I believe that stable basic income level factor can only influence housing and private car buyer desire rises or decreases more than book buyer because book price must be more cheap price to compare housing and private car buyers. Unless, the library needs to buy many books or the publisher needs to choose whom authors' books to buy bulk amount for book stocks. So, in this library or publish books purchase suitation, the basic expenditure budget will influence their books purchase decision. It may be significantly different than the ones are predicted by the standard economic model if more realistic assumptions of human consumption behavioral prediction success in publish, private car and housing three markets.

Behavioral economic method assumes that consumer will compare whether whose benefits are more than costs after they buy the product or consume the service. I assume the housing , and private car consumer is only the who have stable basic income source consumer target. This stable basic income target housing, private car consumers who will evaluate or feel they will earn more benefits than costs to every product in their consumption process, after they will make final decision to choose to buy the product to use or consume the service. Otherwise, if they feel they won't earn more benefits after they buy the product or consume the service in the consumption process. Then, they won't choose to buy the product to use or consume the service. In behavioral economic view point, it indicates their consumption behaviors are depend on comparing the product or the service whether it can satisfy their desire benefits and their desire benefits to the product or service must be more than their consumption cost.

There are four points to apply behavioral economic method to predict each stable basic income individual income spending. They include: motivation, conspicuous consumption, social preferences and crowding theory.

Each stable basic income consumer individual spending amount will be different and it is represent that every high stable basic income consumer must decide to consume any high cost services or buy high cost products to use. Although some economic teachers assume general high income people will accept to spend more expenditures for enjoyment or buy high cost of products to satisfy basic high level necessary expenditures. But, applying behavioral economic analysis, it is not absolute true, some low income people also accept to spend more to buy high cost of products or increasing spending expenditures for enjoyment for their basic necessary expenditures.

The field of behavioral economic can be fined as a combination of economics and psychology that tries to capture human behavior in a more realistic. Understanding each consumer individual consumption behavior, we need to know how who does each decision to influence each consumption choice. Consequently, analysis reaches the conclusion. Every high or low level stable basic income consumer individual behavioral consumption that the microeconomic consequences of a stable basic income of individual consumer target consumption group could be efficiency enhancing, but at the same time incentives about positional concerns could lead to wasteful and inefficient spending to the stable low basic income consumer target group.

● How to apply demand and supply theory to contribute to the stable basic income target housing and private car consumer group's consumption prediction?

What is basic income mean? A basic income is an income paid by a political community to all its members on an individual basis, without means test or work requirement. How to apply behavioral economic method to contribute to the basic income consumption prediction?

I assume high income tax is charged to one high income tax payee , it will influence the high income tax payee individual consumption desires to be fallen, also extrinsic incentives will effort and intrinsic motivation and how the labor market change these variables under and big changes predicting, how income security changes social consumption preferences, e.g. how a big change affects the overall level of status -seeking behavior and this effect with income inequality to influence consumer individual consumption attitude or habit.

How can behavioral economic methods predict housing or private car consumer's consumption decision, in special the stable basic income consumer target group? In any house or private car consumption decisions are involving risk and uncertainty, the standard economic model usually assumes that decisions are based on final condition, regardless of the changes are caused by the results of a consumer's decision.

An alterative mode of how housing or private car consumers make decision and judgement under risk and uncertainty. This situation is often occurred in consumption market.

In behavioral economic view point, it explains how housing or private car consumer's consumption, however, which excludes the stable basic income earn factor can influence the stable basic income earn target consumer group decides to make final consumption decision to compare to the non-stable basic income earn target consumer group. The reasons include as below:

(1) Housing or private car consumers evaluate decisions over gains and losses with respect to some natural reference point, when they feel need to consume, which is assumed to be judgement about a sequence of outcomes are based on changes in wealth, rather than whether how much absolute basic income earn to influence whose living or driving desires.

(2) Thus, behavioral economic theory assumes the housing or private car consumer is the low level of income group in society, but when who feels that he is still gains more than losses when who decides to buy the expensive product, such as house or private car or consumes the expensive service. Then, the low level of income consumer who will accept to buy the expensive product or consume the service easily. Due to whose gains feeling is more than losses feeling, when who buys the car or house product or consumes the living or driving service.

(3) Behavioral economic theory also assumes the taxpayer will pay high income tax in this year. The, even the high income taxpayer can earn high basic income, but due to whom needs to pay high income tax in this year. Then, he/she will reduce much spending, even he/she reduces spending on cheap products or cheap service consumption for enjoyment. This is the taxpayer's economic decision to influence whose consumption behavior, due to the high income tax expenditure factor influences whose consumption behavior to change to be reduced spending expenditures in this year. So, the high income tax taxpayer will not make decision to buy any house or car easily in the year , when he is charged high income tax last year.

● How can apply demand and supply theory raises basic stable income consumer house or private car consumption desire

Economists aim to develop models of human behavior and interactions in consumption markets. But consumers behave in complex ways, such as how to predict consumers to make rational decisions in consumption processes. Moreover, self-consumption control and motivation can vary significantly across different individual consumer, such as house and private car markets.

In order to build useful consumption prediction models, economists make simplifying assumptions, aims to predict how to raise stable basic income housing or private car consumer target group consumption more success. However, behavioral economy method is one kind of accurate consumption prediction method. It can be applied to predict economic decision-making to every house or private car consumer consumption choice more accurate raising whose consumption desire?

I shall indicate how to apply different behavioral economy methods (demand and supply theory) to raise stable basic stable income target consumer group consumption desire in these different consumption situation (house or private car consumption environment) aspects as below:

1. Stable basic stable income housing or private car consumer group consumption great or small amount desire

The consumption of housing or private car products is a fundamental part of consumer's welfare. Basically, every one who has stable basic stable income, who will like to consume any products and services. Even, consumption great or small amount desire won't be depended on whether the person whose income is more or less. It means low income level of people will still like to consume great amount to buy expensive products, such as cheap private car or cheap house or consume , because consumption is human's part of life and basic needs, such as living or driving leisure behavior.

This stable basic income people will like to consume, because they have stable income source when they do not worry about unemployment occurrence to cause them have no enough money to support their life. Otherwise, non-stable basic stable income people won't like to consume because they feel they have no stable basic income source to support their life and they will worry about unemployment occurrence any time. Hence, stable basic income people will have more consumption desire to compare non-stable basic stable income people in any countries usually. Behavioral economic method indicates they feel their economic benefits will be loss if they planned to buy any products or consume any services easily. So, they prefer to save money in bank more than consumption.

1. Demand systems and micro-economic factor influence basic income people housing and private car consumption attitude

Why stable basic income people will like to consume? Because who have more demand, a demand system shows the level of consumer demand for different products and services: e.g. one basic stable income person may refer to the demand for clothes, another the demand for food etc.

How the demand for that particular house or private car product varies with the prices and demographic factor will influence who to accept consumption. Such as stable basic income people who will not consider to decide to buy the cloth to wear or the food to eat if who feel the cloth or food price is even more expensive to compare other kind of cloth or food, even buy the higher price book to read in book shop.

Otherwise, non-stable basic income people who will consider to decide to buy the cloth to wear or the food to eat if they feel that they still have enough cloths to wear or enough food to eat at homes , even these food or cloth price are less expensive to compare others or compare which book price is cheaper. Because they feel they lack stable income effort to support them to consume. Hence, basic stable income factor can influence the consumer's consumption decision.

2. Life-cycle advertisement method can influence book consumer or reader individual consumption behaviors to be increased

Consumer behavior makes strong assumptions about the informational and computational bases of consumer behavior. Generally, consumer behavior is reasonably characterized as the maximization of expected lifetime utility subject to budget constraint and conditional on the available information.

Generally, readers or book consumers prefer to buy any discounted books or it is reasonable that book consumers accept to buy many attractions to persuade them to buy any kinds of bargain discount products. Hence, low bargain discount product is one good behavioral economic principle to encourage or persuade or attract any consumers to increase consumption.

What is behavioral life-cycle model? This model explains reader or book consumer behavior can be persuaded to buy any discounted products by advertisement, e.g. television, radio, newspapers, magazine etc. promotion channels. Because frequent advertisement promotion method can let any consumers often remember the product's brand, discounted price, style, color and image from advertisement content.

So, advertisement can be one part of consumer behavioral life-cycle. For example, when the television audiences often watch TV. Hence, when the brand of product advertisement often makes fun image and discounted message to let TV audiences to remember this brand of product, when they are watching TV. Then, it has possible to persuade any potential consumers to choose to buy this brand of any products or consume this brand of any services, due to its advertisement of discounted sale message is very attractive to every one to let this advertisement audience's attention to remember this brand of products or services are selling or serving in market at this moment. So, it is advertisement image behavior influences audiences to buy the brand's any products attractively and persuasively.

- Consumer confidence is as a predictor of consumption spending in book, house and private car three markets.

Behavioral economists believe it has link between confidence and economic decisions to cause consumers to choose spending, if the consumer has confidence to believe the product is worth to use, then who will accept to buy the product to use, e.g. the book is value to choose to read, the private car is value to drive or the house is value to live.

Concentrated on the conceptualization of confidence and its role in mode in theories of consumption. It also concerns on whether the confidence indicators contain any information beyond economic fundamentals. The concern is whether confidence can be explained by current and past value of variables, such as income, unemployment, inflation or consumption or in other way.

Whether confidence measures have any statistical significance in predicting economic outcomes once information from the above variables is used. Economic variable factor will also influence consumer confidence to decide consumption spending, e.g. real consumption expenditures (income, wealth or interest rate).

Finally, it will identify under which circumstances confidence indicates can be a good predictor of household consumption. Hence, survey is one good measurement method to predict whether how much every household has confidence to spend expenditure to buy the house to live long time or but the private car to drive long time or the book to read long time. Why is survey a good confidence consumption measurement prediction to every household in every country?

The reasons include survey can gather every household consumption habit history data to evaluate whether every survey person has how much confidence to consume the brand of products. Which in most cases correspond to periods where there are large changes in household survey indicators, liking during financial crises or geopolitical tensions to measure or predict whether the country's future good or bad economic condition factor will influence every household house or private car purchase or many books reading desire in the year.

This modelling approach assumes that there is a certain (unknown) in confidence index changes beyond which confidence starts impacting consumption behaviors. So, sample household surveys can show the contribution of confidence in explaining consumption expenditures increases when household survey indicators feature large changes. So that confidence indicators can have some increasing predictive power during the survey investigation period in the year.

Other view point, surveys have been concerned on whether the confidence indicators contain any information beyond economic fundaments. The concern is whether confidence can be explained by current and past values of variables, such as income, unemployment, inflation or consumption or the other way. Whether confidence measures have any statistical significance in predicting economic outcomes once information from different external variable factors to influence the survey household group.

What is confidence in consumption survey ?

Confidence in consumption. For example, to measure whether how much degree of strong inflation in the economy, such as recessions and recoveries will influence the country's household confident consumption in the year. The surveys consumers' questions usually concern on major expenditures and changes in the respondent's financial situation, focus on job availability and current business conditions etc. questions. It is then possible that about consumer confidence depending on the relative performance of the variables that may be more relevant balances, with respect to the factors that determine unemployment and other labor market related issues. It aims to investigate whether those any one of variable factors will influence consumers general loss confident consumption desire in this year.

What is a confidence indicator ?

A confidence indicator is considered as an explanatory variable for consumption together with standard variables used on predicting consumption expenditure. However, the natural real personal consumption expenditure is unexpected and unpredicted easily.

In conclusion, consumption expenditure depends the consumer individual confidence. If the consumer has much confidence to feel this year economic change will be better and he/she is easily to find job, then he/she will accept consumption easily in this year. It seems financial wealth and unemployment etc. economic factors will influence every household consumption desire. So, survey is one kind of good psychological consumption prediction method to predict consumption spending for any country in the year. I recommend manufacturers may choose to apply survey method to attempt to enquire sample survey people to gather data to predict whether what degree of consumption desire to them and find solution methods to solve low degree of consumption desire challenge.

How to apply behavioral economy methods to influence employee individual psychology to achieve raise productivity of long term incentive intention?

Increasing salary is short term incentive productivity method. Behavioral economy assumes labors will choose to do beneficial behaviors to themselves when they feel their work behaviors can earn more benefits to themselves more than their employers in the organizations. Otherwise, if they feel their work behaviors can earn more benefits to their employers more than themselves. Then, they won't choose to do their work behaviors, e.g. raising productivities or work hard. Due to they feel work hard or raise productivities behaviors that only give more benefits to their employers more themselves.

Whether does cheap product price incentive consumption desire to influence effective consumption behavior? Whether is monetary increasing salary payment incentive labors might be willing to work on task? I feel raising labors productivities is similar to raise incentive consumption, which both have similar point, such as increasing salary payment or cheap product price is the main factor to influence incentive consumption or raising productivities. Hence, it seems monetary factor is not the main effort to encourage labors to work hard.

In labor's behavioral economic view point, for example, if an employer pays an employee more doing a task, who might be less willing to work on it, who might be less productive given whose efforts and who may enjoy the task less. If you want your employees to save more for retirement. You may want to give them fewer investment options. If you want them to engage more in a task, you might want offer them an additional alternative, instead of increasing salary to that task. Thus, increasing salary is not only method to encourage productivities of incentives.

CHAPTER TWO

Private Car Market Consumer Behavior

● Why does technological factor raise rental car service needs ?

The automobile industry today is the most lucrative industry. Due to increase in disposable income in both rural and urban sector and availability of easy finance are the main drivers of high volume car segments. Proper understanding of consumer buying behavior will help the marketer to succeed in the market. All segments in Car industry were studied and found that buyer has different priority of behaviors in each segment, where as main driver for car purchase is disposable income. Value for money, safety and driving comforts top the rank in terms of customer requirement; where as perceived quality by customers mainly depends on brand image. This chapter also attempts to consolidate findings & suggestions to overcome present scenario of stagnancy in sales and cultivate future demand for automobile car market.

Due to the growing economic difficulties and environmental concerns that many countries are facing nowadays, car-sharing services are gaining new members every month and they are enjoying wide public attention as an innovative transportation mode that could also contribute to solve pollution and congestion problems of several cities across the globe. The concept is that users are allowed to use a car when needed without having their own, thus providing a flexible alternative that meets different transport exigencies, reducing costs and the negative impacts of private car ownership. Aim was to unveil the characteristics of potential new car-sharing members and the most relevant factors for the growth of the service. For this scope data exploratory analyses of current travel habits, behaviors and attitudes towards the service of the interviewed were conducted. The survey included a significant amount of current members, so an examination of their behaviors is also presented. In general results showed different users' needs and a strong link between travel habits and propensity to forego the use of the private vehicle. The analyses also demonstrated the importance of more information among the users about the potential economic benefits of the service, given their poor awareness of the real costs related to the private car owning. Furthermore it turned out that wider availabilty of the vehicles, a better integration with public tranports in combination with an extensive use of Information Systems are fundamental for the growth of the service.Should You Consider Buying a Used Rental Car? Are the deals on used rental cars from rental-car companies as good as they seem? So, it causes rent car service need increases, instead of new or second hand car purchase need increases in car market. As you might expect, used rental cars have lived a harsher life than other used cars. Miles are piled on at a much faster rate, and renters may not have been the most considerate drivers. So it makes sense that rental-car companies looking to unload their vehicles seek to sweeten the deal for used-car shoppers with lower prices and promotions. For example, Enterprise Holdings, the largest rental-car company in the U.S., gives shoppers seven days to decide whether they are happy with a purchased car. We strongly suggests using that time to have the used rental car inspected by a certified mechanic (about $100). Enterprise and Hertz also offer "no-haggle pricing" and a limited powertrain warranty (covering the engine and transmission) that lasts 12 months or 12,000 miles, whichever comes first.

● Car past driving safe record report performance influences car buyer choice

But some automative analysts believe that shoppers can and should get even more consider used models from automakers with the longest bumper-to-bumper and powertrain warranties, such as automaker buyers of a used Hyundai or Kia get the remaining balance of both warranties, capped at five years or 60,000 miles. When buying any used car, remember that your best choices should have solid CR reliability scores, a clean history report, and the safety features you want. Imagine you are a consumer who is about to purchase a car. You may imagine it to be any consumer (male or female, in full time employment or student, married or single, old or young, rich or poor, children or no children, etc') but be sure to clearly state the personal characteristics you imagine this particular consumer to have. It may also be useful at this point to establish whether you are able to gain information on your imaginary chosen consumer (from sources such as Mintel) so that you have credible sources from which to base your report on. Your report is expected to describe and explain the characteristics that affect consumer behaviour and outline the consumer decision-making process as it relates to purchasing a car for this consumer. You should also discuss the relevance of the decision-making process to Marketers of cars in general and provide recommendations of how they can influence the stages of the decision-making process.

● The car buyer or car renter making decision process

The term consumer behavior includes the customers of specific goods and the people using the goods. It is usually used to refer to any human market behavior and use of products and services. Today, consumer behaviour is a multidisciplinary science that investigates not only the consumer decision-making process and the acquisition of product, but also the further activities of the consumer after the purchase of the product, such as using, evaluating and rejecting the product or service (Blackwell et al. 2001).

Consumer Behavior Incentives

According to the definition given by Wilkie (1994) people buy and consume goods to satisfy their needs and desires. It could be said that consumer behavior is a behavior motivated to meet specific goals, needs and desires. In most cases – though not all – of the consumer behavior, people buy and consume goods as a means to satisfy some of the needs – material and sometimes emotional. It should be noted that consumers motives are not always obvious to third parties and as a result the use of theories and conduct of researches are necessary for better understanding of consumer behavior. In the present example, the woman wants a car to go to work, pick up kids from school and go to super-market. These are her stated needs. The car marketer should find out the emotional needs of the particular customer.

A part of consumer behavior derives purely from functional motives), such as when someone buys bricks to build a house, buys a car to satisfy transportation needs while another part of his/her behavior is stimulated by selfexpressive motives (Wilkie, 1994:), as when someone buys a gift for to thank a family member or buy a car to satisfy his prestige needs. Blackwell et al.(2001),in contrast with this position argue that the needs of consumers should not be divided into two major categories, but in subcategories that should include and explain better the different consumer needs. Some of these needs are the physiological needs, the need for health and safety (as it is the case of the car – safe travels), love and companionship, the need of financial resources, the need for pleasure, the need for the creation of the social image of the individual (buying a specific car brand to enhance personal prestige), the need of possessing (everybody has a car) and the need of information (Blackwell et al. 2001:233-245). At this point it should be mentioned that most consumer behaviors wish to fulfill more than one target or needs, thus not only talking about one motive, but about a group of motives which motivates consumer behavior. In the present example, the groups of motives are transportation, social image and possession needs. In addition, while some motives may be visible to consumers and third parties, others may be more difficult to determine, for example when the decisions that should be taken are more complex and closely linked to the feelings of the consumer.

The activities of consumer behavior

The act of consumer, it should be taken into account the thoughts, feelings, plans, decisions, markets and experiences accumulated by the act of consumption. Certainly, a researcher of "purchasing" behavior who focuses on the act of consumption and does not consider it globally, may omit other equally important activities (advertising, opinions of others, collection of information, evaluation of alternatives, purchase decision, type of payment, product use, etc.) that are contained within it and they are equally important. These activities can be distinguished into deliberate and coincidental. For example, the activity of the decision of buying a product can be described in most cases as a deliberate consumer behavior as it is the case of the car where the consumer has to plan in advance the car purchase. On the other hand, when a consumer visits a store to buy a specific product in mind, she/he sees a multitude of other goods and not a few times he can buy some of these without having a plan. Such consumer behavior may be classified as impulsive. This differentiation is particularly useful to researchers of consumer behavior and advertisers, who understand the mechanisms of behavior more comprehensively (Wilkie: 1994).

The process of consumer behavior

The concept of process which includes various activity stages is a very useful approach to better understand consumer behavior. This process has three stages. The first stage of the activities of pro- buying could include the actions to select the product which is followed by the second stage of purchase of the product – and finally the third stage of the after-purchase, which includes actions such as the depreciation of the product. The activities before buying the car could be search at auto-magazines, advertisement exposure etc., whereas at the third stage there could be activities like the evaluation of technical service etc.

Diversification of consumer behavior

Two elements that could differentiate the consumer behavior of the individual are the the time and complexity of the decision. Time refers to when the decision is taken and the duration of the completion of the process. Complexity refers, to the number of activities involved in making a decision but also to the difficulty of this decision. Buying a car is a complex decision since it involves product and price comparison, ways of payment etc. Since it is a complex decision it is also time consuming. Relating these two concepts, it is understood that the more complex a decision is, the more time is needed for the decision. It is understandable that the more complex a decision is the greater will be the activities of the pre-purchase. In the present case, the activities could be talking to friends, look at car magazines, go to car exhibitions etc. Many times, however, the consumer to avoid a possible delay, which may lead to a not so profitable market – s/he has not seen offers for the product so s/he acts with less detail than he could.

In other words, s/he tries to simplify the decision-making process in the following ways (Wilkie:1994):

1. The car consumer is not always looking for the best carpurchase, but for a good car –acceptable purchase.

2. She/he is driven by information, advice and recommendations of third parties. The opinion of friends and family can play a significant role in the car buying decision.

3.She/he trusts the car brands and car stores purchased in the past driving safe experience and has past driving performance record from many past car buyers remained satisfied with them. The car salesman should check the previous car brands purchased by the customer.

Several times, the process of satisfying needs, is confronted with the simplification of the decision making process. As for example, the purchase of a relatively cheap product which should have the required by the consumer quality standards. Many car consumers face maintaining " the past car safe and driving performance record report knowlege from magazine" on the purchasing process, therefore they can take advantage of these situations.

Roles and Consumer Behavior

A consumer in the decision process and after having made the decision,may have more than one roles, for example she/he can be the person that affects the final decision of the purchaser or user (influencer). She/he could be practicing these three roles at the same time as when shopping alone or when shopping only for himself as below:

The first role is consumer behavior, may influenced by others, so the role of the individual who affects the final decision may be played by people of the individual's wider social environment – a friend / the family or otherwise it could be the salesman. In the present example this woman could be influenced by her husband in her decision. Moreover the role of the user in many cases could not be the purchaser and / or influencer, but a third person who will use the product purchased. It is understandable, that the possible combinations of these three roles could be outnumbered by those already mentioned, depending on the consumer, the external environment but also his personality. The woman, for example, may be influenced by her husband but she has her own personality thus she may choose the car brand that is more suitable to her.

The second role is that consumers mentioned above are born through social interactions. Very few purchases are made driven solely by the "ego" – consciously or subconsciously people's decisions take always into account their social circle. It is also important to note that the roles change during the lifetime of the consumer. For example, a child rarely can be an influencer and even more rarely buyer. The purchases of a childless young man usually involve himself, and a consumer with children buys largely for his family and certainly is influenced by the needs of other family members as it is the case in the present example.

The third role is that Extrinsic (environment) factors can influence Consumer Behavior. It is a fact that the consumer is influenced by his/ her environment, a fact that highlights the ability to adapt to different circumstances, depending always on the needs that should be met. This exogenous influence impacts on the consumer decision-making process. These factors are: Culture refers to beliefs, values and opinions shared by members of the society where people live and has a catalytic effect on people's behavior during their life by putting "limits" in people's understanding on which products and services are acceptable. The subcultures, are groups of people who belong in the broader context of culture and share similar values and attitudes. A subculture could be working women with children Some examples are those of gender, ethnicity, race, age and religion. Also, the social class that someone belongs to is a factor that may influence consumer behavior (Pinson & Jolibert: 1998). Like what is his/her job, income and education level that s/he has.

On above three roles, one of the main factors affecting the purchasing behavior is the family. Especially in Mediterranean societies, where the family institution is still strong, people are influenced by consumer habits as children and later as adults. The social surroundings and the reference groups to which people belong is an equally important factor, since everyday conversations and contacts affect consumer habits. For example, if someone play sports, s/he will definitely be affected by the advice of his/ her coach regarding his/her dietary habits and clothes preferences.

Wood, M. (1998) indicated the external conditions such as inflation and unemployment or an illness in the family are factors that will determine the amount to be spent to purchase a product and when it is best to purchase a specific commodity. The marketing environment in conjunction with the presence at mass media is an area that in recent decades has gained immense power of influence in today's consumer. For example, usually the ads aim to influence consumer for a particular product of a certain brand, while the factor culture does not "suggest" specific brands but more goods for consumption. For example, one publisher decides to sell a one-use textbook to students.The school makes decision to buy the second hand text book, it's decision will be followed this factor: The second hand book author does not receive any royalties and have no economic interest in the text – when the student buys the text, the publisher can earn less royalty income. It's designed to be a "disposable," one-use text in order to keep the price down. (The used book market actually drives up the price of texts – to see why, think of what would happen to car prices if used car sales were not permitted or think of what would happen to house prices if second hand house sales were not permitted). If the country is facing inflation and unemployment or an illness in the family are factors that will determine the amount to be spent to purchase a product and when it is best to purchase a specific commodity, this bad economic environment factor will influence the coutry's second hand houses and second hand private car sale number decrease, even their prices are less than the normal price 50% or more because many people are losing jobs in the year.

In this bad economic environment, how do the used car markets drive up the price of the good? With an used market, the buyer is willing to pay more, knowing that he can resell later. However, without an used market, everyone is forced to buy new cars, raising demand, and thus raising the price of new cars. How to think about these countervailing effects?

However, used books and used cars and second hand house markets , they have similar consumer behavioral characteristics. Are the used books and used cars and second hand houses actually have similar consumer behaviors ? However, used car and second hand house markets , they have similar consumer behavioral characteristics.

I believe that seond hand book market is different to second hand car or second hand house both market. In used book market, the professor and his publisher have a monopoly on the new textbook, but no one controls the new car market or the new house market. Therefore, if people keep reselling text, the publisher will use their monopoly and raise the price of new books to compensate. In contrast, car manufacturers and house sellers can't do so due to competitive pressure. Imagine that there are two kinds of people, rich and poor, and no market for used books. Rich people are willing to pay more for new textbooks. Poor people cannot afford to buy new textbooks. In the absence of a market for used books, poor people will not buy textbooks. Imagine now that there is market for used books. Poor people are now able and willing to pay second hand textbooks. And rich people now have someone to sell the books too once they are done using these books. A market for second hand textbooks raises the price of textbooks because some people are not able and willing to buy new textbooks but are willing to buy second hand textbooks. In the absence of such a market, they'll spend their income on other goods that they deem more important. Think of it otherwise this way. In the absence of a market for used textbooks the full value of a textbook is not exploited because some people who would wish to trade with one another cannot trade with one another. From what I can understand, in the context of the used books market, lets assume that there is set, finite amount of demand for the books. When there is a used books market, the demand first goes to the used books market and finishes up the supply in that market. The remaining demand then goes to the new books market (the professor/publisher). To compensate for the loss in demand, the publisher would therefore have to raise prices of the new books.

Now for the cars market, when there is no used cars market, everyone is indeed forced to buy new cars which raises demand and consequently price. However, you are assuming that cars are a necessity and that the demand transfers 100% from used cars to new cars. Some people maybe only purchasing cars from used cars market because they see the value in the lower price. When there is no longer a used car market, if the price of the new car remains the same, then people would deem that price to be too expensive since they are unable to resell it later on and ultimately choose not to buy at all or opt for alternatives. This actually reduces demand. To capture the market of such consumers, the car companies would ultimately reduce prices to get the market share. This is from the Bertrand competition model point of view.

● Non price factors influences automobiles buyers' needs or desires
The market for automobiles has always been a large part of the countries GDP. Not only that, it also has been a big part of the International Trade through imports and exports. Even though it is a huge firm, there are many automobile companies and each company has its own contribution to the automobile market. This has created competition in the market. That's why, the general price of automobiles move together up or down. The factors that affect the general price of automobiles. Of course, these factors are non-price determinants of demand and non-price determinants of supply. I will also discuss the price elasticities for the market of automobiles.

Factors affecting demand and supply
Automobiles are considered luxury goods with many years for duration to last. Therefore, the demand for automobiles is positively related with the economic growth of the countries. Whenever there is extra income, people spend it on luxury goods including cars. And to provide these people with automobiles, firms produce cars. Of course, there are important factors affecting the demand and supply. These factors are the non-price determinants of demand and supply.

The demand view to car market
1. Weather factor influences car buyer demand
First of all, the tastes of people should be explained. With so many options available in the car market, consumers began demanding cars with more features two decades ago. For example, from 1990 to 2007, the demand for

air conditioning in automobiles increased rapidly . This caused demand for automobiles without air-conditioning to decline whereas for automobiles with air-conditioning to increase. As of late, however, people are becoming more aware of global warming and that the automobiles is one of the causes. Although their number is not great, still there are consumers using canceling their purchase in order to contribute to solve global warming. All these changes in the consumer tastes affect the demand for automobiles. And when the demand is law, the price of cars falls down until the supply restores new equilibrium price.

2. The price of substitutes factor influences car buyer demand

Secondly, the price of substitutes must be explained. The number one substitute for automobiles, or rather the usage of automobiles, is the public transportations. If the ticket price is noticeably low, many people may choose to use public transportations. This is especially true for crowded cities and for millions of students around the world. Consequently, this will affect the demand for automobiles negatively. As followed, a fall in demand will cause a fall in price. It is important to note here that because of the global warming, governments are taking necessary steps to encourage people to use public transportations rather than their individual vehicles. Thus, it is more probable that the effect by the price of substitutes will be high.

3. The complementary goods to automobiles factor influence car buyer demand

Next, the complementary goods to automobiles must be discussed. The gasoline is the famous complementary good to automobiles. If the price of gasoline rises, as it was in 2003, the demand for cars will fall noticeably. Reversely, if the price of gasoline falls, as it used to be many years ago, the demand for automobiles rises. But according to the US Department of Energy, the price of oil (which is used to make gasoline) has been always rising (with very small exceptions). It means that the effect by the complementary goods will be negative on the demand for automobiles in the future, add to that the movement by the 'global-warming-preventers'.

4. The income distribution factor influence car buyer demand

Then income distribution must be explained. Income distribution is commonly from the rich to the poor. With the increased income level, the poor may be able to purchase an automobile, provided other factors don't influence him against his decision. Therefore, the demand may in fact rise the rich still buys and the poor now can buy. (From this perspective, demand for hatches or luxury houses may decline because these are the luxury goods for the rich!)

5. Future expectations factor influences car buyer demand

Finally, future expectations must be explained. The future expectations range from common belief to individual belief that the price will rise or the supply will decrease. In either case, people purchase more or less automobiles. For example, currently, people think that the low demand for cars due to the slowdown in the world economy will bring the prices down. Therefore, they may have been postponing their purchases. However, determinants of the demand are not the only factors affecting the prices. To any change in demand, supply responds, too. Therefore, people postponing their purchases may not win as much as they expect.

The supply view to car market

The supply of automobiles is an enormous process. Currently, there are more than 176 car manufacturers in the world, including GM Uzbekistan in Asaka, Uzbekistan. These companies are always on the lookout for bigger market share or new markets. They watch the demand for the products and try to respond to any change in it as soon as possible by either increasing or decreasing the supply. However, changes in supply are not only to respond to the changes in demand. There are factors, which affect the supply that are independent of the changes in demand. These factors, known as 'non-price determinants of supply', are mentioned in subsection 'factors affecting demand and supply'.

1. Production costs factor influences car buyer demand

First of all, the production costs must be discussed. Speaking from the economics terms perspective, the costs of production. For example, if the workers' union demands higher wages, or government imposes a new regulation protecting the environment or raising the interest rates, the automobile supplying companies incur higher cost of production. Because demand is constant (temporarily, at least), companies make changes in the supply, which directly affects the price level.

2. The profitability of alternatives factor influences car buyer demand

The profitability of alternatives is another important determinant and must be explained. However, it must be understood that the process of manufacturing automobiles is extremely complex and requires huge and expensive equipments. So, the usual explanation in the economics 'can switch to the alternatives' does not work here. However, usually the companies produce different automobiles, in other words, they have diversified their product line. For example, they produce light vehicles and trucks, or large automobiles and small ones. So if the price of one type of automobile changes, it affects the supply of other types of automobiles; the companies use up all their resources to supply more of the car whose demand is higher and less of the car whose demand is low (or unchanged).

3. The aims of the car producers factor influences car buyer demand

The aims of the car producers should be discussed. Traditionally, it had been assumed that the only aim of the companies is to make profit. However, it has been studied later that the car producers sometimes may have other aims than profit. Sometimes, the other aims can affect the supply level and this, in turn, affects the price of the car product. For example, if we assume that the automobile companies are at high competitive market and want to destroy each other, they may aggressively increase the supply level in hopes that the lowered price of automobiles forces the weaker companies out of business (because the increased supply would have caused the price to drop down noticeably.)

The future expectations to the car producer is the another aim must be explained, too, as it affects car producers in the same way as car consumers. For example, if the automobile companies believe that the price of gasoline is going to be cheap, (gasoline and automobiles are complementary goods), they will store their car and oil products for the future. This action causes the supply to be low and, consequently, the oil and car price level to be high. Or for example, if American automobile manufacturers believe that Japan intends to export a huge number of cars to the North America, American companies increase their supply, which drives the market price lower. (This is also an example for 'the aids of the producers' because here the aim of the producers plays some role in affecting the automobile price.)

4. The unpredictable events or nature acts factor influences car buyer demand

Finally, the unpredictable events or nature acts play another role. They are flood, earthquake, terrorist attacks, etc. Naturally, the unpredictable events can affect all the non-price determinants of both demand and supply and, through them, affect the price. If anything happens within the company, i.e. earthquake or fire destroying the car equipment, the company must replace the damaged parts – a big change in the cost of carproduction. Or if anything happens in oil producing countries such as Iraq-Kuwait war in 1990, Iraq war in 2003, this has some indirect effect on the price of automobiles, because, as mentioned, gasoline and cars are complementary goods.

● Factors that determine the price elasticity of supply of automobiles
Price elasticity of demand
Price elasticity of demand is the responsiveness of the quantity demanded to a change in the price. It is calculated using this formula: Pe.d=Δ(%)Qd/Δ(%)P. And, according to the elasticity rule, there are three cases:

Elastic demand = E>1
Inelastic demand = E<1
Unit elastic demand = E=1

Some economists believe that he price elasticity of demand for automobiles is 1.8. in car market in common. It is inelastic demand: a small percentage change in the price leads to a big percentage change in the quantity demanded. Therefore, demand for automobiles in the graph on the right is flatter.

Price elasticity of supply
The price elasticity formula is similar to that of demand. Instead of percentage change in quantity demanded, we use percentage change in quantity supplied: Pe.s=Δ(%)Qs/Δ(%)P. Obviously there are many factors that determine the price elasticity of supply of automobiles. First of all, changing the level of supply is not an easy process. So the response of supply to a change in price is slow.
Having analyzed the factors of both demand for and supply of automobiles, we can say that there are many factors that can cause the changes in the price of automobiles. The non-price determinants of demand such as people's tastes and expectations, price of substitutes and complementary goods have all played role in affecting the price of automobiles. Similarly, the non-price determinants of supply such as the costs of production, profitability of alternatives, producers' expectation and aims have played role, too. Since the price elasticity is more than 1, we can conclude that it is elastic.

● What's the effect of the used car market on car price and seond hand book price similar consumer behavioral characteristics?
While justifying when one book shop sells a one-use textbook to one student reader , this book shop is similar to one car seller sells a used or second hand car to one car buyer selling behaviors. I shall explain that why

second hand or used book is similar to second car or used car selling or consumer behaviors, they have similar second hand book or car purchase behavioral characteristics as below:

A word about the Kearl text. I do not receive any royalties and have no economic interest in the text – when you buy the text, not a single penny goes to me. It's designed to be a "disposable," one-use text in order to keep the price down. (The used book market actually drives up the price of texts – to see why, think of what would happen to car prices if used car sales were not permitted.)

How does the used car markets drive up the price of the good? With an used market, the buyer is willing to pay more, knowing that he can resell later. However, without an used market, everyone is forced to buy new cars, raising demand, and thus raising the price of new cars. How to think about these countervailing effects? Are the used books and used cars market actually analogous like the professor suggests? The professor and his publisher have a monopoly on the new textbook, but no one controls the new car market. Therefore, if people keep reselling text, the publisher will use their monopoly and raise the price of new books to compensate. In contrast, car manufacturers can't do so due to competitive pressure. Imagine that there are two kinds of people, rich and poor, and no market for used books. Rich people are willing to pay more for new textbooks. Poor people cannot afford to buy new textbooks. In the absence of a market for used books, poor people will not buy textbooks. Imagine now that there is market for used books. Poor people are now able and willing to pay second hand textbooks. And rich people now have someone to sell the books too once they are done using these books.

A market for second hand textbooks raises the price of textbooks because some people are not able and willing to buy new textbooks but are willing to buy second hand textbooks. In the absence of such a market, they'll spend their income on other goods that they deem more important. Think of it otherwise this way. In the absence of a market for used textbooks the full value of a textbook is not exploited because some people who would wish to trade with one another cannot trade with one another. If there wasn't a used good market($\rho=1$), the editor would have to satisfy a constant demand, and you solve it just for one period (which will stay the same afterwards). The price for new books will be below the one you calculated above. On the consumer (student) side, they would have greater resistance to buy books that cannot be resold. There would be pressure placed on the professor to find cheaper alternatives. In other words, there should also be an effect on total demand, on top of the competition with old books. – Brian Romanchuk Apr 25 '17 at 21:20

In used car and second hand book similar consumer behavioral characteristics view, a buyer wants a way to make revenue back on the initial investment of a car, if this isn't possible (a used car market doesn't exist) then the car buyer may find another investment opportunity and avoid cars altogether. However, without a used car market, demand for new cars would increase, presuming cars are a necessity, and so therefore would the price. The price of new cars could possibly reduce if there is a used car market as the dealers will want new stock leaving so that they don't stop trading.

From what I can understand, in the context of the used books market, lets assume that there is set, finite amount of demand for the books. When there is a used books market, the demand first goes to the used books market and finishes up the supply in that market. The remaining demand then goes to the new books market (the professor/publisher). To compensate for the loss in demand, the publisher would therefore have to raise prices of the new books.

Now for the cars market, when there is no used cars market, everyone is indeed forced to buy new cars which raises demand and consequently price. However, you are assuming that cars are a necessity and that the demand transfers 100% from used cars to new cars. Some people maybe only purchasing cars from used cars market because they see the value in the lower price. When there is no longer a used car market, if the price of the new car remains the same, then people would deem that price to be too expensive since they are unable to resell it later on and ultimately choose not to buy at all or opt for alternatives. This actually reduces demand. To capture the market of such consumers, the car companies would ultimately reduce prices to get the market share. This is from the Bertrand competition model point of view.

In actual fact, Bertrand competition are not seen and huge companies work with each other more often then they engage in price wars. Now consider the Cournot competition model where inverse demand for the good is given as P = a - bQ (i.e. law of demand - when the price goes up, demand must go down ceteris paribus.) Since there is no used cars market, then demand for new cars market has gone up, the car companies produce more output (Q has gone up), ceteris paribus, P will come down. Just to reiterate, if there is a used cars market, then total output (Q) would be lower, therefore P will be higher.

Note that both the Bertrand and Cournot model dictates that prices will go down without a used cars market, just that the Cournot model reflects the actual situation clearer.

- Technology influences the car user demand change for the Auto Industry

The growth of organized car rental industry is continuously growing with support of technology. The car customers in the present era are using mobile apps to book a cab at anytime and from any place in urban areas. The pricing strategy of cab operators had been positively influencing customers to book a cab instead of traditional mode of transportation like autos and local buses etc. Like most of the industries the car rental industry had underwent lot of transformation with internet technology. The consumers are able to access book cabs at competitive prices because of tough competition among the organized cab operators. In this regard the present paper briefs about the behavior of consumers while booking cabs. The variables like coupon redemption, innovativeness and price consciousness.

1. Quality > Affordability

Quality can, of course, mean different things to different people and different markets. It's important for auto brands to dig further into this and find out what aspects (security, aesthetics, reliability) are most important for their target audience. For example,'Innovative products or services' in auto brands than those in other countries. Brands must do their research to ensure the product they're producing meets the quality standards in the regions and communities they're targeting. There's more to a car than getting from A to B.

2. Sustainability and renewables

Sustainability was not particularly popular , although many people globally named renewable energy as one of the biggest transformative technologies of the next year. This presents an interesting contradiction – while many think renewable energy will change the world in the next year, few of us are prioritizing sustainability when it comes to choosing auto brands. This could be because vehicles that don't harm the environment are very much still in the minority, and could be seen as too expensive or not practically viable for consumers. As climate change protests grow in number and size, it seems like the time is now for auto brands to move on this point.

3. The importance of friendly customer service
Globally, friendly customer service was an important attribute, with 10% of people choosing it as the most important attribute for an auto brand. When we looked at social data, negative conversation focussed mainly on people's experiences when cars go wrong – dealerships, warranties, fixing things and things not working were big topics of discussion. Clearly, when people are shopping for a vehicle, or when things go wrong with the vehicle they have, there's an opportunity to garner favor with customers with warm interactions.

4. Non-manual driven auto car invention
We were keen to find out what consumers thought of the prospect of self-driving cars as we head into 2020. While many clearly think they're a way off, we found that 9% of consumers globally think self-driving cars will be the most transformative tech of 2020. Meanwhile, of all the transformative tech we studied, self-driving cars are the third most hyped tech we studied on social. Looking at responses by country, those in the US were most likely of all the countries to vote for self-driving cars, while responses from Spain were least likely of all the countries likely to choose this option.

5. The innovative behavior of consumers helps to download mobile apps and further motivates car users to redeem coupons
Clearly, consumers are getting more interested in sustainability in the auto industry, even if they don't currently value it over affordability and quality. The consumers who are price conscious are likely to redeem coupons while booking cabs. The innovative consumers are interested to adopt for new technology like use apps for booking cabs and other services. The redemption of coupons is motivating factor for consumption of cab services. The consumers have got habituated for mobile apps to book cabs and they are also feeling safe with regard to organized cab services. It is also observed from the study that middle aged adults are consuming cab services compared to other age groups.
There is stringent competition in the organized cab services industry therefore organization need to motivate consumers through coupons. The innovative behavior of consumers helps to download mobile apps and further motivates them to redeem coupons while booking cabs. The results of this study are consistent with earlier research studies because it is found that price conscious consumers are likely to redeem coupons. The modern consumers are innovative and at the same time they are price sensitive therefore coupon redemption helps for customer retention. The brand

image also plays a vital role in customer retention apart from offering coupon.

Reference

Wood, M. (1998), "Socio-economic status, delay of gratification and impulse buying", Journal of Economic Psychology, Vol. 19, pp. 295-320.

CHAPTER THREE

Publish Market Reader behavior

Nowadays, publish market includes these main book service aspects to let readers enjoy reading interest, such as ebooks online reading channel, traditional book shop books purchase channel, library books lending service. I shall analyze how these books leading or borrowing and send hand or new books purchase choice to influence readers reading behavioral need change.

● Library Services in the Digital Age

The internet has already had a major impact on how people find and access information, and now the rising popularity of e-books is helping transform Americans' reading habits. In this changing landscape, public libraries are trying to adjust their services to these new realities while still serving the needs of patrons who rely on more traditional resources. In a new survey of Americans' attitudes and expectations for public libraries, the Pew Research Center's Internet & American Life Project finds that many library patrons are eager to see libraries' digital services expand, yet also feel that print books remain important in the digital age.

The availability of free computers and internet access now rivals book lending and reference expertise as a vital service of libraries. In a national survey of Americans ages 16 and older:

1. 80% of Americans say borrowing books is a "very important" service libraries provide.
2. 80% say reference librarians are a "very important" service of libraries.
3. 77% say free access to computers and the internet is a "very important" service of libraries.

Moreover, a notable share of Americans say they would embrace even wider uses of technology at libraries such as: Online research services allowing patrons to pose questions and get answers from librarians: 37% of Americans ages 16 and older would "very likely" use an "ask a librarian" type of service, and another 36% say they would be "somewhat likely" to do so.

Apps-based access to library materials and programs: 35% of Americans ages 16 and older would "very likely" use that service and another 28% say they would be "somewhat likely" to do so.

Access to technology "petting zoos" to try out new devices: 35% of Americans ages 16 and older would "very likely" use that service and another 34% say they would be "somewhat likely" to do so.

GPS-navigation apps to help patrons locate material inside library buildings: 34% of Americans ages 16 and older would "very likely" use that service and another 28% say they would be "somewhat likely" to do so.

"Redbox"-style lending machines or kiosks located throughout the community where people can check out books, movies or music without having to go to the library itself: 33% of Americans ages 16 and older would "very likely" use that service and another 30% say they would be "somewhat likely" to do so.

"Amazon"-style customized book/audio/video recommendation schemes that are based on patrons' prior library behavior: 29% of Americans ages 16 and older would "very likely" use that service and another 35% say they would be "somewhat likely" to do so.

When Pew Internet asked the library staff members in an online panel about these services, the three that were most popular were classes on e-borrowing, classes on how to use handheld reading devices, and online "ask a librarian" research services. Many librarians said that their libraries were already offering these resources in various forms, due to demand from their communities.

These are some of the key findings from a new national survey of 2,252 Americans ages 16 and older by the Pew Research Center's Internet & American Life Project and underwritten by a grant from the Bill & Melinda Gates Foundation. The interviews were conducted on October 15-November 10, 2012 and done on cell phone and landlines and in English and Spanish.

- Public priorities for libraries

Asked for readers or students thoughts on which services libraries should offer to the public, majorities of Americans are strongly in favor of:

Coordinating more closely with local schools: 85% of Americans ages 16 and older say libraries should "definitely" do this. Offering free literacy programs to help young children: 82% of Americans ages 16 and older say libraries should "definitely do" this. Having more comfortable spaces for reading, working, and relaxing: 59% of Americans ages 16 and older say libraries should "definitely do" this. Offering a broader selection of e-books: 53% of Americans ages 16 and older say libraries should "definitely do" this. These services were also most popular with the library staff members in our online panel, many of whom said that their library had either already implemented them or should "definitely" implement them in the future. At the same time, people have different views about whether libraries should move some printed books and stacks out of public locations to free up space for tech centers, reading rooms, meeting rooms, and cultural events: 20% of Americans ages 16 and older said libraries should "definitely" make those changes; 39% said libraries "maybe" should do that; and 36% said libraries should "definitely not" change by moving books out of public spaces.

Americans say libraries are important to their families and their communities, but often do not know all the services libraries offer. Fully 91% of Americans ages 16 and older say public libraries are important to their communities; and 76% say libraries are important to them and their families. And libraries are touchpoints in their communities for the vast majority of Americans: 84% of Americans ages 16 and older have been to a library or bookmobile at some point in their lives and 77% say they remember someone else in their family using public libraries as they were growing up. Still, just 22% say that they know all or most of the services their libraries offer now. Another 46% say they know some of what their libraries offer and 31% said they know not much or nothing at all of what their libraries offer.

● Changes in library use in recent years

In the past 12 months, 53% of Americans ages 16 and older visited a library or bookmobile; 25% visited a library website; and 13% used a handheld device such as a smartphone or tablet computer to access a library website. All told, 59% of Americans ages 16 and older had at least one of those kinds of interactions with their public library in the past 12 months. Throughout this report we call them "recent library users" and some of our analysis is based on what they do at libraries and library websites. Overall, 52% of recent library users say their use of the library in the past five years has not changed to any great extent. At the same time, 26% of recent library users say their library use has increased and 22% say their use has decreased. The table below highlights their answers about why their library use changed:

- How people use libraries

Of the 53% of Americans who visited a library or bookmobile in person in the past 12 months, here are the activities they say they do at the library:

73% of library patrons in the past 12 months say they visit to browse the shelves for books or media.

73% say they visit to borrow print books.

54% say they visit to research topics that interest them.

50% say they visit to get help from a librarian. Asked how often they get help from library staff in such things as answering research questions, 31% of library patrons in the past 12 months say they frequently get help, 39% say they sometimes get help, 23% say they hardly ever get help, and 7% say they never get help.

49% say they visit to sit, read, and study, or watch or listen to media.

46% say they visit to use a research database.

41% say they visit to attend or bring a younger person to a class, program, or event designed for children or teens.

40% say they visit to borrow a DVD or videotape of a movie or TV show.

31% say they visit to read or check out printed magazines or newspapers.

23% say they visit to attend a meeting of a group to which they belong.

21% say they visit to attend a class, program, or lecture for adults.

17% say they visit to borrow or download an audio book.

16% say they visit to borrow a music CD.

These survey indicated that African-Americans and Hispanics are more likely to say libraries are important to them and their families, to say libraries are important to their communities, to access the internet at the library (and feel internet access is a very important service libraries provide), to use library internet access to hunt/apply for jobs, and to visit libraries just to sit and read or study. For almost all of the library resources we asked about, African-Americans and Hispanics are significantly more likely than whites to consider them "very important" to the community. That includes: reference librarians, free access to computers/internet, quiet study spaces, research resources, jobs and careers resources, free events, and free meeting spaces.

When it comes to future services, African-Americans and Hispanics are more likely than whites to support segregating library spaces for different services, having more comfortable spaces for reading, working and relaxing, offering more learning experiences similar to museum exhibits, helping users digitize material such as family photos or historical documents. Also, minorities are more likely than whites to say they would use these new services specified in the charts below.

Statistical analysis that controls for a variety of demographic factors such as income, educational attainment, and age shows that race and ethnicity are significant independent predictors of people's attitudes about the role of libraries in communities, about current library services, and about their likely use of the future library services we queried. In addition, African-Americans are more likely than whites to say they have "very positive" experiences at libraries, to visit libraries to get help from a librarian, to bring children or grandchildren to library programs.

- Second hand book market

Why is used car market similar to second hand car market consumer behavior ? When one publish decides to sell one used book. It will concern that how much the used book sale price and it won't need to concern the author can receive any royalties and have no economic interest in the text – when you buy the text, not a single penny goes to me. It's designed to be a "disposable," one-use text in order to keep the price down. (The used book market actually drives up the price of texts – to see why, think of what would happen to car prices if used car sales were not permitted.) How does the used car markets drive up the price of the good? With an used market, the buyer is willing to pay more, knowing that he can resell later. However, without an used market, everyone is forced to buy new cars, raising demand, and thus raising the price of new cars. How to think about these countervailing effects? It seems that second had book and car markets , they have similar characteristics to influence consumer behaviors.

Are the used books and used cars market actually analogous like the professor suggests? The professor and his publisher have a monopoly on the new textbook, but no one controls the new car market. Therefore, if people keep reselling text, the publisher will use their monopoly and raise the price of new books to compensate. In contrast, car manufacturers can't do so due to competitive pressure.Imagine that there are two kinds of people, rich and poor, and no market for used books. Rich people are willing to pay more for new textbooks. Poor people cannot afford to buy new textbooks. In the absence of a market for used books, poor people will not buy textbooks.

Imagine now that there is market for used books. Poor people are now able and willing to pay second hand textbooks. And rich people now have someone to sell the books too once they are done using these books. A market for second hand textbooks raises the price of textbooks because some people are not able and willing to buy new textbooks but are willing to buy second hand textbooks. In the absence of such a market, they'll spend their income on other goods that they deem more important.

Think of it otherwise this way. In the absence of a market for used textbooks the full value of a textbook is not exploited because some people who would wish to trade with one another cannot trade with one another. From what I can understand, in the context of the used books market, lets assume that there is set, finite amount of demand for the books. When there is a used books market, the demand first goes to the used books market and finishes up the supply in that market. The remaining demand then goes to the new books market (the professor/publisher). To compensate for the loss in demand, the publisher would therefore have to raise prices of the new books.

Now for the cars market, when there is no used cars market, everyone is indeed forced to buy new cars which raises demand and consequently price. However, you are assuming that cars are a necessity and that the demand transfers 100% from used cars to new cars. Some people maybe only purchasing cars from used cars market because they see the value in the lower price. When there is no longer a used car market, if the price of the new car remains the same, then people would deem that price to be too expensive since they are unable to resell it later on and ultimately choose not to buy at all or opt for alternatives. This actually reduces demand. To capture the market of such consumers, the car companies would ultimately reduce prices to get the market share. This is from the Bertrand competition model point of view.

● Is It Best to Buy or Borrow Books?

In gneral, reader will choose either to visit library to borrow books or visit book shop to buy book. In any readers' reading behavioral choice process, they will compare whether the book shop has same book to sell or library has same book to borrow, if the book can be sold or borrowed in shop or library. Then, the reader will compare the price between the library's the book list price and the shop's the book sale price. Hence, if the library's the book list price is more expensive to compare the shop's same book's sale price. Then, the reader will choose to visit the book shop to buy the same book in possible. So, his earlier borrowing the book desire will be changed to visit the book shop to buy the same book because the book shop's same book's sale price is cheaper than the library's same book. Unless, the reader does not visit the book shop , so he believes that the library's the book can not be sold from any book shops.

One major positive of buying books is more money in the pockets of authors, who — unless they're someone like Harry Potter creator J.K. Rowling — tend to need all the sales they can get. Plus you're giving business to bookstores. Then there's the pleasure of adding another title to your home shelves — where the book is always available for reading, for impressing guests with your superior taste in literature.

But taking out titles from your local library has advantages, too. It's free — an especially nice price in these grim economic times. It's eco-friendly, because many people eventually peruse the same copy. And it can lead to more reading, because there's a deadline for when the books need to be returned. Sure, you can renew a book. But I try to avoid that. If I borrowed four library books the month before, I'll stay up late a few nights before the due date to finish that last one. I read approximately 10 more novels a year that way. Last but not least, library users are supporting an important government institution at a time when many right-wingers want to close or privatize almost everything that's not making a profit for greedy corporations. America needs democratic places that welcome everyone, not just people with lots of money.

I first came across this comparison on a popular sales psychology website [link below], and it got me thinking... how do these kind of (genius) persuasion techniques apply to your career as an author? You see, whatever people might say, books – especially ebooks – are cheap. Most self-publishers who sell books on Kindle (or wherever) set the bar at $2.99 – $5.99 per title. And I just know you break out in nervous sweats at the thought of charging more than that. I know I do. But price isn't the only thing readers care about. In many cases, it isn't even their top priority. Raise your hand – ever dropped your book prices down to 99c in the hopes of picking up some much-needed sales? I know I have. But the main problem isn't to do with price. $2.99 or $3.99 or $5.99 isn't a lot of money. It just isn't. The problem is all about POSITIONING.

Car market is similar to book market. In car market, that is, making your prices seem like a good deal. And that's where your sales message comes in. In the case of the car advertisements above – the sales messages focus on what's important to the prospective buyer and frame it as a benefit. The Rolls-Royce drivers want opulence and calm. The Land Rover crowd want

power and ruggedness (which they associate with a noisy engine).
In education and car markets, Think about it like this – millions of people spend $50,000 – $100,000 on a college education. Or $30,000 on a new car. Or $500 on marketing and advertising for their business. Or $200 on a new cover design for their book (you can substitute your own numbers – but you get the idea). And this doesn't feel like a bad deal. Because you're getting what you expect at the price you expect to pay for it. You trust the person or business selling to you. It feels like a good deal, and you're more than happy to pay.
Which brings me to my main point. There are three types of reader in this world:
– First, those who will buy ANYTHING you publish without even thinking twice.
– Second, those who will NEVER buy from you.
– Third, those who aren't ready to buy... yet.
Hence, any paper book shops or publishers need to consider that they must have ebook publishers and libraries to be their competitors. Any readers can choose to go to libraries to borrow to read or pay visa to buy the epublisher's ebooks to read from internet. So, technology had influences any readers' reading habits to change from traditional paper book reading method to ebook reading method. Technology factor will influence readers or book buyers their reading behavioral change. So, any authors' paper books prices can not be raised rapidly , even their prices can not charge more than ebook prices. Otherwise, readers or paper book buyers can choose to read any ebooks to replace paper books from internet channel. Because ebook publishers have more effort to replace any paper book publishers, when paper book readers are influenced to accept to apply internet channel to read any ebooks in popular. So, traditional paper book publishing will change to ebook publishing market in the future.

● Online vs offline book shop different devlopment trend

Nowadays, online book publishing is one kind of popular sale method to global publishing. For example, Amazon publish is as a business model with many potential advantages, relative to a physical operation. It held out the potential of lower book inventing and distribution costs and reduced overhead. Consumers could find the books, they were looking for more easily and a variety book topic choices could be offered for sale. It can accept and fulfill orders from almost any domestic location with equal ease. And most purchasers made on its site would be exempt from sales tax. One Amazon strategy hand, it would have to make its returns and redress processes transparent and reliable, and offer other ways for clients to learn, as much about the book possible before buying. Future online book market development trend, such as Amazon, Barnes & Noble etc. online book shops. How closely would their clietns find book ordering, as a substitute for visiting book stores?

In fact, Amazon is global the largest ingle online booksellers and sells many other products. Otherwise, Barnes & Noble, have been market share diminsh obviously. In the future, Noble & Barnes both will have their market share diminish continue obviously. There are also many fewer specialty re lowest. Hence, it seems online and offline both publishing methods will be competitive. It brings this questions: What is the trend between online book sale channel, its size relative to offline book sales channel, growth rate and the charcteristcs of reders who by online in the future? How book market's online channels are economically different , due to e-commerce's effects on online book market and supply fundamentals? How an online book sales channel might be expected to change equilibrium market outcomes?

I believe online book channel based sale activity varies considerably on these aspects: Sales in manufacturing printing cost, online sale services and online demand print book sale book topic choices. Such as author online advertising, change more or less sale price, online paper book shippng cost, visa card discount or online book shop member card discount book purchase, what welfares to online book buyers are.

Why readers chooce to buy books from internet habitally? In tradition, online book buyers habitally hope to use the internet to buy. Generally, they have these characteristics: They hope to use the internet to buy electronic books at home, they enjoy to read electronic book from computer, it is in any regular capacity , not ncecessarily to visit book shops to find books to buy and they can search any electronic from internet, electronic book is convenient to read from computer or laptop when they catch transportation or going to anywhere. Usually, internet users are higher income, more educated and younger. It seems that education is a sizeable determinant of who is online, even controlling for income. However, gender does not seems to be a factor in explaining internet use. Moreover, many of book qualitative patterns are seen for online book purchases in general are observed for electronic book products on on demand printing book products in particular.

Predition in future, many of the traditional online products , such as electronic or print on demand books, computer hardware , electronic airline tickets, saw more modest , but still substantial growth. In the future, online sellers trend to be newer online book stores and have less brand or reputation capital to signal or famous brand quality. These factors can create in online book sellers, which also often involve delay. However, there are many reasons for online book purchasing. The most obvious is that readers don't have opportunity where unobservably inferior point of electronic or demand on print book purchases.

● Pricing strategy in online and offline
book retailing

The book price represents consumer behavior on price. On one hand, the model contains two probability fuctions which render consumers' reservation prices for each individual channel. On the other hand, it is based on numerous book distribution which represent probabilities from and to each online or offline book store separate channel. Price strategy of book sale concerns how readers select a particualr book? Both offine and online book information seeking price strategies point out the challenges for information systems development. Hence, book price decision based on readers‘ age, e.g. children book price will be chealer than adult book price, due to children book content is usually simple and papers page is less. Otherwise, adult book content is more complicated or difficult to understand and page number is more than children book page number. However, online book store disadvantages are that : information system still often fail in supporting the users in causal leisure situations. In order to improve online book search system. Online book stores need to be better understood user strategies and performance and translate them into purposeful features.

A common analysis approach is to compare price and user strategies and interactions in the digital environment with those that occue in similar physical environment. If online bookstores hope to decide more reasonable electronic books or on demand printing books sale prices to compete with offline bookstores. Since, the physical environment (in this particular case bookstores) usually preceds the development of digital environments, processes and strategies from interaction in the physical environment have already stabilized and experiences can be translated into patterns for digital information system development. Thus, some only digital electronic bookstores , such as Amazon publish' disadvantages are : It lacks physical bookstore environment sale experiences. Otherwise, some owning themselves physical book and online book sale environment bookstores, bookstores that can compare only either paper books or electronic books bookstores to predict what the reasonable sale book sale price more easily. Are these differencs between online/digital book discovery environments and offline (neighborhood bookstore) services? Are researching recommendation strategies differences between observable in online and offline book search sessions? In general, interactive users studies based on user interactions in a ISBS developed web-based book discovery information system are aggregated cross multiple researcher groups. In order to provide a realistic book discovery environment, book collection should be large and comparable to other book discovery systems ,such as online book sale. For example, Amazon library book collection is used consisting of approximately 1.5 million books. Each book contains general metadata (title, authors, publisher, publication , year, etc.) subject metadata (classification, code), subject headings , user generated content (Amazon publish user reviewer, library thing user tags).

● How does India book market trend?

Thus, I believe that online or offline bookstore different book research method will also influence readers' preferable book choices, then their choices behavior will influence how many times to find the book easily. If the online or offline readers can find the book topic or author name or contents etc. information easily. Then, the sale chance of the book will increase. Thus, price can increase more. For high population country, e.g. India, China . Does it have more sale chance, due to many people are living in these countries? What us online book store trend in India? Online book can let readers to buy new books and old books from internet, rent or borrow books from internet or access it in the form of e book, e.g. Amazon publish is the big player of online book business in India today. India where dynamic technologies like mobiles are prevalent, e-book readers may soon make into average household. Some of publishing houses which predicted that it would be long journey for e –books to become part of life needs to India readers. Thus, India will be one potential e book market. India is the third biggest market for English books. However, there are challenges of online bookstore in India. IN fact, online book market has changed the way reading consumer use internet for knowledge. Nowadays, people prefer e books are accessible anywhere, any time for creating flexible and secure online bookstore for online bookstores that need to concern to sell their e books to India markets because India readers shall concern visa card payment method where it is safe to pay to read any e books from internet.

Besides, online information searching has touched every field of human life. In the future, it is possible that purchased via mobile are clothing/ footwear and e book or on demand print books. Also , due to e book is one kind of popular reading product to be enter India market. Currently, the online book market in India is offering exciting and renewed services to the internet users. India readers can accept to buy old books to read from online sale channel. Thus, India will be one new second hand online book store market to follow developed countries, such as US, UK etc.

- Trend and development in the global book market

Under the influence of internet, new media , social networks. The way in which search to satisfy our needs. Internet is the high technological search method to change at the level of products and services, such as e book (electronic book or demand on print electronic paper book) and online e book rent service , online library e book borrowing services. Thus, in the future, global book market will be popular on concentrating selling e books or online print on demand paper books more than general walk in offline book shop paper books sale only method. Due to, internet changes traditional readers' reading habits to enjoy to read e books from mobiles, laptops, desktops more than paper book reading. Thus, the global book market will be predicted online electronic book sale format more than visiting walk in book ship sale format. The digitalization of information enables us to bring into discussion today contents separated from the physical, materials, paper shapes of the book. Today, books could be found online, read online for free or downloaded as an e book in English or any other language. Practically, the book has changed from paper to electronic book. In until , the internet and the e book , the changes were extremely slow. Today, digitalization produces rapid changes to the entire system of printing, distribution and reading books. Hence, the global book market trend will be the major implication on publishes, distribution, authors and book consumers. The online competition brings major changes to traditional distributors, the bookstores, the author of independent distributors noticeable decreased. The number of big distributors' stores will decrease. For example, Amazon publish is the best known global selling books online. Although, it can sell e books and printing on demand paper books both from internet channel conveniently.

In conclusion, e book market will dominate global online electronic book sale market and the e book publisher number will increase. As the same time, the visiting walk in offline book shop number will decrease, due to readers have accept to use laptops, mobiles to read electronic books from internet channel more than reading paper books. It implies paper book publishers need to change sale method, e.g. adopting internet to sell print on demand paper books, or reducing paper book sale price to attract e book readers to choose to buy paper books to read.

- Web vs School campus book store development trend

Why do students choose to buy textbooks online? What factors motivate students choose online textbooks purchase? Nowadays, many online book retailers, such as Varsity books.com and Bigword.com ,. Amazon publish.com are now capturing more of the textbook online store market. What is motivating this behavior changes to student market , instead of children story market, entertainment or travel or sport book market etc. topic market. What causes students to choose purchase textbooks online ? Can likelihood to make purchases online by predicted by various social and personal characteristics of consumers? The online textbook purchase growth is allowing online retailers to capture a substantial portion of sales in some sectors. What motivates consumers to shop on the web? But, what if these factors are nor significant , such as better product availability, lower cost, as is that case when comparing on offline textbook purchasing. There is no significant price advantage to buy textbook online, it is there an availability issue, given that textbook can be purchased in the campus store (Foucault et al., 2000).

I shall assume that precious positive online purchase is positively correlated with the likelihood of an individual purchasing textbooks online. Hence, it influences why readers choose to buy textbooks online again. Following , other factor web consumers are likely shop online to save time and/or money, but what of those consumers who shop online when an equally time and cost efficient alternative is present. With regard to textbook purchasing, the time invested in researching for the appropriate books is likely to be similar, regardless of whether the student bookstore or through an online textbook. With regard to textbook purchasing, the time invested in researching from the time invested in searching appropriate books is likely to be similar: regardless of whether the student chooses to shop in the campus bookstore or through an online textbook retailer.

If time from purchase until use counts, online textbook shopping could be considered less time efficient than its offline counterpart. Due to the readers need to turn on computer to link to internet to read electronic books or wait the print on demand to buy paper books from the electronic book store web site to wait the paper books to post to the online book buyer's home. Otherwise, offline bookstores can reduce time spending to wait the books to be posted to the buyer's home, after who pay money to take the paper book from the bookstore immediately. So, the non-waiting post book issue is still the text bookstore's strength to attract students to buy.

● Prediction of direction of electronic books future trend

What is future trend of electronic book publishing development? To answer this question, we need to know what benefits of (electronic books) can attribute to human's needs. Nowadays, electronic books (e-books) are one way to enhance the digital library with global 24 hours a day and 7 days a week access to authoritative information, and there enable users to quickly retrieve and access specific research materials easily, quickly and effectively. Evenm some ebooks publishers choose to let readers who can borrow ebooks to online readers to read from online libraries to earn profit. For example, Amazon publisher lets every Amazon readers only pay about US$5 per month. Then, who can borrow unlimited ebooks to read from Amazon publisher private online member library website convenently.

Thus, it is one ebooks online borrowing strategy to compette with offline book stores and public library and school library in publishing industry. Due to offline book stores lack borrowing books services to any walk in readers. However, some countries' publich libraries also have similar ebooks borrowing to read services. An an ebook providers' electonic online libraries, online computer library center has been involved in the selection, catalogue and distribution of ebooks. Library users can able to remotely search, locate and checkout ebooks from the library's online public access catalogues. Thus, ebook publisher will have another public library competitor which can provide similar ebook borrowing service to online ebook readers from public library websites.

It means ebook publishers need to adopt any attractive ebook library sale borrowing service strategy to attract public library readers. However, as with any new opportunity, new challenge utilizes the internet opportunity to deliver new book content is no exception, Integrating ebooks into the digital library has created challenges and opportunities for librarians, publishers and ebooks providers for librarians in this ebook library borrowing service market to earn extra ebook lending service income. Because, online borrowing service library can have ebooks borrowing service, then why online ebook readers need to choose independent ebook publisher individual borrowing book service website to replace traditional public library paper book borrowing service. The reasons possible include that the readers can borrow ebooks to study from ebook publisher individual library borrowing website at home conveniently, but it is possible that they can not find any paper books to borrow from public libraries which are the same ebooks to be borrowed from any one ebook store to read, also ebook publishers can let whose ebook borrowers to borrow unlimited ebooks to read and there are longer extend borrowing ebook return days more than public libraries borrowing book return days and ebook readers have no penalty when they return ebooks too late and they can choose to pay little borrowing ebook charge in the month, if who do not expect to borrow any ebooks in the month, who can choose to stop to pay borrowing ebook charge in the month. Hence, they can choose to continue to borrow unlimited ebook numbers from ebook publishers and they are permitted to return ebooks longer time to compare traditional public libraries. For example, when the ebook reader pay only US$5 ebook library service fee to the ebook publisher in the month , then who can borrow the number of ebook up to 50 maximum number in the month as well as who can return the all ebooks to the ebook library within 60 days, it is longer return days to compare traditional public libraries. If the ebook reader can not return all these ebooks after the return day of 60 day. They can permit to extend more 60 return days. After this another 60 return days, they only need to pay US$5 penalty to the ebook store. Thus, it is one attrative ebook library borrowing service strategy in this competitive book publishing industry.

There is no doubt that the same trends that adopts ebooks and e-readers to US ebook publishing market are having a similar effect in other countries as well, such as Mobile ebook or laptop ebook technical development of reading devices that provide an reading experience similar to that of reading an actual book, the increasing penetration of the internet in all areas of life, which is significantly changing reading patterns and reading behavior. The increasing extent to which ebook or demand on printing book consumers are open to new technological reading trends, for which in particular that availability of attractive mobile devices, such as smartphones, portable games consoles, and MPS players are responsible to ebook reader tools.

Future trend will be that publishers and authors need to build close digital cooperation relationship. Publishers, bookstores and device manufacturers should take the opportunity to provide the market now with innovative ebook publishing products. And authors should explore opportunities for digital distributions and support publishers in their efforts to publish content. Publishers should also design a giving strategy and attractive ebook sale website that attracts customers without undermining the value of content. A well-thought out pricing strategy may also help publishers and content gain new customers, those who would not have purchased a traditional book , but may be inclined to buy an ebook that costs less, offers additional features , and works on a digital device . They already own there, usually the ebook price compares to traditional paper book price which have similar content, ebook price will be cheaper them the similar content of traditional paper book sale price.

In the future, ebook publishers will need to position themselves as content providers, and not just the suppliers of physical books. They will have to make content available on multiples media, in multiple formats, on multiple platforms. This content may not be limited to the text of a book itself, it may also include videos and games. This additional content may lead to incremental revenue.

In fact, the only lesisure activities more popular than reading books were watching television, listening to music such the radio and reading newspapers and magazines. Thus, every one should need to choose to enjoy to do what kinds of leisure activities every day. For example, if one person chooses to spend much time to either watch television or listen the music and radio or read newspapers and magazines in the whole day. I believe that he will spend less time to read book in the day. Then, it implies that ebook or paper book readers , the paper book or ebook buyer number will be decrease, due to they spend less time to read or without any reading behavior in the day. Thus, how to persuade every one to feel that reading book habit is attractive or important which can be one factor to influence the paper or electronic book readers, even electronic or paper book buyer number. Thus issue will be an attractive topic to concern for every ebook or paper book publisher on book publishing industry. If these both kind of publishers can persuade any person to feel reading book habit can bring benefits to themselves. They will spend less time to leisure activities. Then, ebook or paper book sale number or ebook borrowing service income will raise in the future. Thus, these both kinds of publishers need to concern how to persuade people to choose to spend some time to read books habitually every day. Consequently, psychological factor will be one important direction to raise book buyer number in publishing industry.

● What are the factors to influence sales and marketing strategies for publishers?

I feel that how to predict book buyers which is driven by book buying experience and the publisher's credibility (loyalty) factors which will influence the any book buyer whose make final decision to buy the book from the publisher. As a publisher, a major goal is to extend whose readership and extend whose readers‘ influences, but where to start? How do publishers understand and serve diverse readers and decision makers in different countries? Whether can readers find the kind topic of book from publishers only, when find the kind topic of book from the university libraries or public libraries? Hence, due to offline and online publishing industry competition is high, global publishers will need to develop a sales plan to satisfy readers' reading taste. For publishers need to conduct book exhibition activities, visit different author's decision makers to research what who like to write negotiate terms to publish books with individual authors, secure sales and manage orders etc. different regulations of publishing to every author.

I recommend online or offline publisher ought concern how to publish every book before they decide to sel their every electronic book or paper book to any countries' readers. The marketing strategy includes to develop plan every book sale projection, SWOT (strengths, weaknesses, opportunities, or threats) to every book to be published to the country's readers to implement the plan. Book sales program, email communication marketing, lead generation to analyze the results, eg. every book purchasing trends, customer profiles, marketing sementation for every book to follow up and bedrief: Measuring ROI, setting priorities and develops tastics, finally customer needs analysis foe every book sale, it includes GAP analysis, ebook online library visits numbers to experience the ebook and focus groups. The, it is cycle to the develop plan again. Thus, if the publisher can have a better understanding of pricing strategy plan which can create price plan to be strengthed changes or cancelled for every paper book or electronic book sale marketing price strategies. Bringing potentially and disastrous reading experience to readers , this factor can be one good method to increase reader number and book sale price and sale number method. Then, the ebook or paper book publishers can make more accurate ebook or paper book sale price to every sale market, e.g. US or UK which is better book sale market, which kind of book can be the popular to these either market, whether UK readers like to read ebooks more or US readers like to read ebooks more or US readers like to read paper books more or UK readers like to read paper books more. Thus, the ebook or paper book stores can gather these data to analyze whether what every book topic sale price is more accurate to achieve the highest sale number and income.

Consequently, more appealing offerings can be developed to broader every publisher's audience and enhanced whose every publisher's image, segments of reader research, e.g. reader age, book reading taste. This is a measure level of penetration of journals and identity opportunity for growth GAP analysis marketing strategies will be popular methods to future book publishing. Based on first hand, expensive visiting and surveying librarians around the world, examing factors unique to each country and culture and make to recommendations integrate in every publisher's communication plan. For example, ebook trends pecentage of ebok spending in online ebook borrowing libraries is a publishing extra income from ebook borrowing readers. It is such one part of the overall electronic book market share income in the electronic book publishing market. In conclusion, internet technological innovation can bring new publishing business chance to ebook development , but it also brings competition to traditional paper book stores. So, paper book stores need have good marketing strategies to win their new ebook competitors.

Analysis of factors influencing online newspaper reading behavior

Nowadays, online newspapers will be popular to let readers to read any newspapers' news from internet. It showed that for online newspapers reader's intention is influenced by performance expectancy, habit and the habit of reading a print newspapers. So, newspapers consumer personal reading behavior was influenced by intention and habit. Some reading behavioral researchers showed some reasons to explain why traditional paper newspaper readers will like to change habits to study online newspapers.

Hence, changing reading habit will be one factor to influence traditional paper newspaper reader individual reading behavior changes to online newspapers reading habit. In fact, high technological communication media will influence mobile phone and internet both new communication media causes. These new communication medias will bring new print electronic media causes, such as print newspapers, online book products. Some of traditional paper newspaper readers will choose to read any news from online newspapers. The reasons include free charge, reading at home in convenient, not need go out newspapers, online newspapers do not need the reader's hands to touch the black word paper newspaper to be dirty, and waste less time to buy every day to achieve economic benefit.

Every online newspaper reader will have this factor to influence whom to change traditional paper newspaper reading habit. The factor shows that attitude has a direct effect on intentions, and is influenced by performance expectancy and effort expectancy or related personal online reading acceptance conceptions. Because of whose acceptance of online newspaper reading attitude is as an important in technology user online newspaper reading attitude was included.

Additional, every online newspaper reader self-efficacy and anxiety are expected to be minor issue to influence the online newspaper reader to change whose attitude to choose not to internet tool to read of an online newspaper. However, different age reader either he/she is young or old age factor will have influence whom to choose online newspaper to read, e.g. old age readers will feel difficult to apply internet technology to read newspaper, otherwise, young age readers will feel easy to apply internet technology to read newspaper. So, the old or young age traditional paper newspaper readers, when the acceptance new technological online newspaper to them, they will adopt online newspaper reading attitude to replace traditional paper newspaper reading habit more easy. So, their acceptance new technological of online newspaper reading attitude will have a direct effect on online newspaper reading intention and are influenced by both paper and online newspapers reading enjoyment performance expectation and online newspapers reading effort expectation, when their expectations were needed to be satisfied more these past traditional paper newspaper reading experience. Moreover, past paper newspapers reading behavior and habit should be noted. Then, these two expectation factors will encourage or persuade the traditional paper newspaper readers change whose reading attitude, reading habit and reading behavior to read online newspapers. Hence, the online newspaper readers' psychological factor will influence whose traditional paper newspapers readers whose reading behavioral changes. Also, it means that expectation factor will influence the traditional newspaper readers to change whose counter intentional paper newspaper reading habit.

However, online newspaper will bring much knowledge to compare traditional paper newspapers , e.g. real newspapers news data, more meaningfulness news, providing the nature of visiting a news website, which can let online news readers can feel different read model primary on frequency with relatively little spread in the amounts of time spent at the site.

What are the main factors to influence online newspaper reading behaviors? Same testing indicates for moderation by the online newspaper age, gender and online newspaper reading experience will bring the online reading newspapers habit influence. The testing also indicates male gender and young age group , this group likes to apply internet to find or seek or search any news matters. Hence, this internet user group will bring to have interest to read newspapers from internet channel. The reason is possible because this young male internet users like to contact new technology, e.g. internet. They think the online newspaper is useful and it is more useful to read the online newspaper to compare to paper newspaper.

The two reasons : liking to contact new technology and feeling the online newspaper is more useful which can support why young male online internet users feel to expect reading online newspaper expectancy were more concrete.

Additional online newspapers usefulness are more considered on unclear concept to explain why this reader group feels more like to study online newspapers. What exactly is the usefulness of reading an online newspaper?

The testing also indicated that some online newspaper readers responded to use the online newspaper to feel natural, it showed to be related to attitude as well as to habit , which seems to hold face validity as a natural feel can be considered on attitude on the online newspaper. So, online reading attitude and online reading habit can reflect why man young male like to read online newspapers more than paper newspaper reason.

Another reason indicated that when the young male readers want to read the news, the online newspaper is an obvious choice for him/her. So, many online newspaper young male readers had felt online newspaper is one another newspaper reading choice to replace traditional paper newspapers.

In conclusion , free charge online newspaper is not the main factor to influence both traditional paper newspaper readers to change their reading habit to choose online newspapers to read suddenly. There are other factors to cause them to choose online newspapers to read, such as more usefulness feeling, contacting new technology, online reading habit, positive online reading attitude etc. different psychological factors which will have more influences to cause their paper newspaper reading habits to be changed. Hence, the free price economic gain actor must not only one main factor to persuade readers to choose online newspapers to read.

● How electronic versus traditional print textbook influence of university students' learning behavior

When one university student was accepted by electronic text book learning channel to replace traditional paper text book learning channel (methods). Electronic text book will bring what positive or/and negative influence to impact whose learning behavior changes. For example, electronic text book learning method will bring positive impact to raise the student's examination grades and perceived learning scores or it will bring negative impact to fall down the student's examination grades and perceived learning scores. The mean scores indicated that students who choose to text books for their learning aim. It will have significantly higher perceived affective learning performance and examination results. Thus, the purpose of student learning and teacher teaching method, every university needs to examine whether it is efficient to raise student learning effort to replace paper text book learning method in any learning environment, e.g. many students and one teacher classroom learning environment or the independent student learns himself/herself at home learning environment or library learning environment.

Can text book reading tool bring absolute advantages to university students or bring some disadvantages to them? When a student needs to apply e-text book to learn, who needs access e-text book in a static location, such as a computer or on a mobile device. So, the e-text book in a static location factor, it will have influence to each student reading or learning behavior to bring negative and/or positive both impacts.

The e-text book was distributed on a CD and installed on a located computer. This limited the user to accessing the e-textbook in a single location and eliminated the potential access to the e-text book on due to the lack of mobility. So, it seems that the location of limited to e-text book will bring negative impact to let the student can only learn in a fixed location because he/she will feel difficult to move heavy computer to other places to learn more than on paper text book. So, e-text book location can not allow the student to leave the classroom to learn more easier if he/she had chose to use to computer to install the CD to learn in the classroom. Supposing the student 's teacher needs the student often to leave the classroom to discuss any matter suddenly, it is not very convenient to the student to use e-text book to learn because he/she can not move the computer to leave the classroom with him/her easily. Then, it will be possible to influence the student can bot be attention to read the e-text book, when the teacher needs the student to leave the classroom (none book bringing) to discuss any time any time immediately. Otherwise, if the student used one paper book to read/learn in the classroom, if the teacher needs whom to leave the classroom often to discuss immediately. He/she will feel convenient to learn because he/she can bring the light paper book to leave the classroom to discuss with the teacher in any location easily.

Hence, it seems e-text book learning will bring not convenient fixed location learning environment to every e-texting learning student in classroom, when, he/she needs often to leave the classroom to discuss with the teacher any time.

Other disadvantage of e-text learning will bring students feel difficult in possible. In the past, some learning researcher experiments indicated results demonstrated that student participants in both groups had similar recall and ability to reinterpret information suggesting that retrieval of information is not effected by kindle e-book reader e-text book, a tabled computer e-text book or a print version.

Hence, it seems that e-text book can not help or assist recall the student's learning memory to remember the e-text book content more easier. Due to it is one e-text book machine, the student will fell to difficult to find any unclear or important information in any page(s) to write for learning/reading record more easier than one paper text book.

Another disadvantage of e-text book is the inefficacy or inefficient reading challenge to the e-text book reader. The efficacy of e-text books in a higher education environment will be one interesting discussing question. Passage length is one difference that impact the results. Studies involving shorter reading sessions indicated no substantial variance with respect to reading comprehension and understanding.

Conversely, studies involving longer reading passages indicated prior comprehension, when reading longer e-text , eye fatigue and mental workload are also concerns. Hence, e-text book reading will be possible to let students feel eye fatigue and mental workload in their reading process.

Due to machine e-text book words are more small size and unclear more than paper text book words to print to let students to read every words or sentences in computer. Consequently, studies indicated that e-text book readers need to spend much nervous and time to read longer and poor comprehension in whole e-text book reading process. When, university students need to spend time to read longer e-texts from computers. For example, they need to choose to reads hundreds of papers of e-text books on a screen, whether on a computer or handheld electronic device compared to print versions may contribute to eye fatigue. The consequence, eyestrain and mental fatigue could be poorer comprehension and have a poor eye, nervous health influence and every student's e-text learning behavior can bring negative reading habit to whom, when every one need to apply desktop or laptop or mobile electronic tools to read any words from e-textbooks. Hence, it seems e-text book reading method has possible to bring poor health challenge to every student.

So, abovc all thcsc c-lcarning rcading factors to bring this qucstion: Docs e-learning influence the student's negative reading behavior to cause poor final examination grades results? In fact, every student needs to change whose traditional learning method from paper text book reading habit or reading behavior to e-text books. He/she needs to change whose reading habit. He/she must need to spend long time to accept how to adopt this kind of new technological reading method as well as effect may change through a new technological learning experience itself and impacts the acquisition of knowledge leading to reading behavioral change.

As I indicated the e-learning will bring poor health and poor nervous negative influences when the student often needs to apply electronic product to read long time. So, it will be possible to influence the student health to be poor to bring examination low grades results in possible be cause he/she has poor health to exam.

It is possible that it has relationship to influence the student to exam low grade between e-learning habit and poor health causes. The reason is based on that efficacy of textbook format is defined grades. I assume that all these negative e-text book reading factors can influence every e-text book reader's health to be poor when he/she needs often read e-text book s to cause long time reading habit. So, I mean that e-text book reader individual health changes to poor, it is only depend on how long time e-text book reading habit factor. So, if he/she only spend less time to read e-text books and he/she also has habit to read paper books sometimes. Then, he/she won't be influenced to be poor from e-learning method easily.

It means that it has none direct relationship between less time e-text book reading habit and low examination grades result. Hence, low examination grades result to the student, it only depends on long time e-text book reading habit and the student's long time e-text book reading habit needs to confirm that whose long time e-text book reading habit causes poor health to the student effect. Why do I believe that efficacy of textbook format can influence the student's examination grade? Based on above analysis, the e-text book reading format and paper book reading format is very different. For example, the efficacy of textbook is very different between paper text book reading format and electronic text book reading format. Such as one sickness student needs to spend more nervous to read one e-text book more than one paper text book . This reason is because machine reading method is difficult to compare paper reading method. When the student has sickness, who must need to spend more time and nervous to read one e-text book more than one paper text book. If my assumption is right, then the e-text book sickness reader's reading efficacy to each paper must be poor to compare the paper text book sickness reader , due to the sickness e-text book reader needs to spend long time and much nervous to read each paper more than he/she chooses to read one paper book. When he/she is sickness to finish whose reading . Due to his/her memory will be poor and tries, when he/she feels sick, so whose reading effort must be poor when he/she needs to apply computer tools or mobiles to read.

● How to change future e-reader
study habit to feel better

Nowadays, publishers, internet bookstores manufacturer e-readers have high expectations for digital future of book industry. If they expected e-book publishing industry success, they need to considerate how to assist to future e-readers to let them to feel whose reading habit to be better in order to persuade or attract them to choose to read e-books more easily, due to doctors indicated that long time e-books reading will cause eye poor health and tired and poor nervous reason in possible and paper book price competition and more topic choice reason. It is one value consideration question that e-book publishers need to considerate.

For example, in the US Amazon publish has improved the reading market by producing e Reader that is easy to use and making it easy for clients to purchase a wide variety of books at competitive prices. It will bring digital reader technology as an opportunity to open new target markets and create new e-readers. The question is how Amazon publish , such as e-book publishers change future e-reader reading habit to feel to choose e-books reading method is better than paper books reading method. The successful factors may include as below:

E-book reading market is similar to e-music listening market. They need every e-book reader and/or digital music listen listener to discover why to apply this kind of new digital technology reading or listening method which is better to enjoy to read every e-book content and/or listen every digital music song in order to adopt new listening and/or reading digital technological learning habits or experiences. So, this new digital technological reading or/and digital music listening process, every e-book reader or digital music listener needs to learn how to adopt this kind new digital reading or/and listening products to change from his/her traditional paper book reading or/and CD/DVD music song listening method to this new technological digital reading or listening methods from computer tool channel.

In this changing habit process, every e-book reader or/and e-music listener needs to spend some time to learn how to apply internet technological tool to help whose to read digital book or listen digital music from computer channel. So, he/she must attempt to change whose habit from traditional paper book reading habit and/or CD/DVD listening music habit to e-book reading habit and/or e-music listening habit.

Furthermore, e-book publishers also need to know whether which kind of book topics are be favorable popular to be chose to read for either student reader target to read or mature age reader target to read or old age reader target to read. Who will purchase the topic to read to be e-Reader? Will they be designed to appeal to be a group of e-reader customers or only to those who have a high degree of comfort with technology to enjoy e-reading method? Will people who read once in a time be purchased by the small group of e-reading clients who buy and read a high volume of e-books?

What reasons, readers will choose to read the topics of e-books more than paper books? Will publishers be able to use e-books and e-readers to extend the many different age e-reading clients, e.g. young, mature, retirement, old, student age e-readers? Will publishers ever more to all readers are only choose digital e-reading model habit or who are a half digital e-reader and a half paper book reading habit clients to them?

Hence, one successful digital publisher needs to consider how to persuade every traditional paper book habit readers to change their reading habit to read digital e-books from computer. Because changing habit is one challenge to influence the e-book publisher 's e-book reader number. How to persuade the paper book reading habit readers to change whose attitude to choose to read e-books , it is one considerate question to every digital publisher? Some readers may feel difficult that who needs to learn new knowledge how to read e-books from computer tool, e.g. old age reader group. This reason will influence they still choose paper books to read in habit. So, any e-book publisher has responsibility to teach new digital technological knowledge learning method to let the e-book desire readers can feel easy to apply internet to read e-books from computer tool.

Another factor is e-book price, normally every e-book price will need to be sold cheaper to compare the similar paper book topic in order to persuade paper book readers choose to buy the similar topic of e-books to read more easily. Because if the reader discover the e-book topic is similar to the paper book topic contents, but the e-book price is charged high than the similar paper book topic content, then he/she will possible to choose to buy the similar paper book topic to read.

Another factor concerns how to raise e-books attraction. E-publishers will need to position themselves as content providers, and not just to be similar to the suppliers of physical books. They will have to make content available on multiple media, in multiple formats, on multiple platforms. This content may not be limited to the text of a digital book itself, it may also include audio, video, image and sound speaking digital books to attract e-readers' attention.

Another factor is that I recommend e-book publishers need to let all e-book readers to feel reading e-books are leisure time habit to let them to enjoy life every day in popular. Intention is such as good tool for anyone to apply to entertainment, for example people linked using internet to read books, watch movies, play video games from computer tool. They are some main points. They have same main points. They tend to spend leisure time with electronic media, such as apply internet to watch television which is such as to apply internet one more choice to assist readers to read e-books from computer media tool conveniently at home.

However, this is one example e-book attraction point to e-reader. Every e-book needs have e-pub files to allow readers to control the size of the text or their computer screens. If the e-reader feels the text is small size and computer screen is small size in difficult to read. Then, he/she can use mouse tool to change the e-book text number to be high number, e.g. from 18 to 20 or more number and he/she can apply mouse tool to move the computer screen to be wider more easily. Hence, it is e-book attraction point to e-book readers to feel when he/she feel the text is small size to read in difficult. Otherwise, every paper book print text(word) size is fixed, all word size can not be changed to read and every paper book wide size is also fixed. All it is every paper's unattraction point to every paper book reader.

Consequently, every e-book publisher needs have its attraction point to let its every e-book reader feels it is different to the other paper book publishers. It needs to solve these challenges to let its every reader to accept to choose its e-book reading channel. The challenges may include how to let the e-reader feels its e-book reading media can provide a more comfortable e-reading experience to compare other e-book publishers' reading media, how to let its e-readers feels its all e-books can provide one precise and stable e-book reading characteristics, how to let its ebook readers to feel its every ebook displays does not require any background lighting and one easy to read, even in direct sunlight environment, and it e-reading tool can spend less energy from laptop battery or desktop electricity to compare other e-book publisher reading tool, it means that the e-book publisher's ebook reading tool can provide a recharged power desire which can be used for several thousand pages or seveal weeks e-reading function. Hence, it the e-book publisher's e-book reading tool can provide more clear words and text image as well as less electricity consumption function to let every e-reader to read to compare other ebook publishers from laptop, destop or mobile media. Then , the ebook publisher's competitive effort will raise to win its other ebook publishing competitors. However, any ebook publisher needs have attraction points to persuade its ebook readers to read its any ebooks feel comfortable and providing fun ebooks choices and easy to read its every ebook text more clear if it expects to win its competitors in ebook publishing industry.

- Factors influence child reading habit

Reading failure is a serious educational problem to influence every publisher success because if the child chooses to buy its books to read, but its child readers can not feel its books can help them to assist their learning success or failure examination or low grades result. Then, it will influence its child reader number to be reduced. However, the factors cause reading failure, it is not only considered to the publisher's poor book content quality factor, it can include the other factors such as: It is simply be attributed by poverty, immigration or the learning of English as a second language. What factors will influence child read in wrong habit to bring reading failure, even learning failure in effect? It is one question to every publisher needs to know in order to avoid they feel failure examination emotion after read their e-text books. Hence, how to design every text book content is one important issue to ever publisher.

A study by Yankelovich found most children are reading, but they are not reading enough. It indicated only about 3 in 10 children can be classified as high frequency readers who read books for fun ever day. Age 8 children are less to see benefits t oreading for fun, girls are more likely boys to have positive attitude about reading and feel fun. The benefits of reading are evidenced by the attitude of high frequency readers to achieve future learng success. More than 40% of children ages 5 to 8 say they are high frequency readers, by ages 9 to 11 that proportation drops to 29%. Almost half of the 15 to 17 year old (46%) are low frequency readers compared with 14% of 5 to 8 year old age. So, this study investigation reflected that building good learning habit has relationship between frequency reading and feeling fun to read to every child. It seems that one fun content book can attract the child to read the whole book all content really. So, publisher needs to consider how to design and write attractive content books to let every child to read.

What factors cause every child feel barriers to read? Some investigations indicate that young children tend to maintain high expectations for success, even in the face of regarded failure, when old students don't, also to older students feel failure following high effort appears to carry more negative inplications. Moreover, all students individual attitude about their capabilities and their interpretation of success and failure is further factor to affect their willingness to feel fun to read in themselves learning proceses.

So, it concludes this fun book content design method can persuade young people feel fun to read really. Moviated readers hold positive benefits about themselves attitude or reading habit which will bring positive and attractive reading emotion to influence them.

What are the book publishers and teachers' responsibilities to improve student individual negative habit to have positive reading habit or positive learning attitude? The ultimate goal in teaching and reading book is to raise students comprehend te ideas in a piece of text as they need. So, any publisher has responsibility to publish one fun and meaning book in prior, because every teacher will teach whose students by the text book content. If the text book content is fun and attractive and meaning, then the teacher can teach to let every students to learn more easily.

Training every student owns good reading habit which can help whom expand their thinking skills, learn to concentrate and enlarge their vocabulary and effectively better their learning environment. The good reading habit ought be trained from the child stage in beginning. So, when the child has is growing up, when he/she is needed to go to primary, secondary, even university to study, he/she had been built good reading habit from the publishers' fun and meaning book content influence in order to let they further learn any new knowledge to feel more easily. So, publishers have responsibilities to sell fun and meaning content books to let every child to read to raise whom reading interest to further young and mature learning stages.

However, the problems, children experience learning to read are often not related to their ability to learn, but to their awareness. Their ability to hear the English language and their expose to the English words. So, repeating to spell the English words will assist the child to raise memory to remember to write the English words more easily. So, book publishers have responsibilities to express every book content to attact child readers to feel interest or fun to learn to remember to spell every word as well as teachers have responsibilities to train students how to hear the words, he/she assist every child to learn to spell the English word more easily. So, teachers ought often speak every word or speak every sentence loudly from every book content to let students to listen easily in order to let they can raise every word memory more easily.

Consequently, instead of child's parents and child himself/herslf has responsibility to help the child self to build good reading habit, teachers and book publishers have also responsibilities to help them to build good reading habit because fun and meaningful books which bring more attraction to influence every child to read, when the book is fun and meaningful , then the teacher can follow its content to teach whose students to attract them to learn more easily. However, the good reading habit includes elements of reading comprehension to every book content , such as: identifying and summarizing the main idea, comparing and contrasting, identifying supporting facts and details, making influences and drawing conclusions, predicting outcomes, recognizing fact and opinion, identigy cause and effect recognizing sequence of events, identifying story / case elemetnts, such as main characters, settings, conflict, and resolution, identifying the another's purpiose and point of view, interpreting literary devices, such as imagery , symbolisms.

Hence, publishers ought to follow above these elements to design their every book content in order to let child readers to feel fun and meaningful and easy to read. Because reading comprehension elements will be one important factor to train every child or mature student reader to build good reading habit or attitude more easily and effectively in order to raise their future good reading effort in their every learning stage in success.

CHAPTER FOUR

Housing Market Buyer Behavior

Can internet influence property buyers' house locations, prices and house design and property developers' choices ? can technology sale method change property buyers' behaviors ?How and why behavioral economic method can predict house buyers house purchase need or desire whether the country's house buyers their house purchase need or desire will increase or decrease in the year. I shall explain the reasons as below:

What does behavioral economy mean ?Think about supposing you plan to buy a house. You may have decided to simplify your decision making by opting for the house price, living environment, such as air and noise pollution, income level, school, public library, public park, public swimming pool, transportation facilities etc. different factors to influence you house purchase decision in the location. You may then have visited the house location to view its environments before you decide to choose the location to buy the house to live. But the decision making process did not stop there, as you now had to customize your model by visiting from different house location . You aim to compare whether anywhere location(s) can let you to feel the location is better to let you feel to live.) Instead the house location and environment factor, you were still considered the house appearance and design and comfortable feeling features you really needed. At this stage, most property developers will show a base model with options that can be changed according to whether the house buyers their preferences are environment, house design, house price, facilties before they decide to buy the house to live. The way in which these different location of house choices are presented to house buyers will influence the final house purchases made and illustrates a number of concepts from behavioral economic (BE) theories.

First, the base model shown in the customization engine represents a rational choice to any house buyers' purchase decision usually. Usually, house buyers, they will visit the house location to feel its living environment, entertainment facilities supply, transport facilities supply and house design and comfortable feeling to decide to buy the house to live, instead of income factor in house market. The more uncertain house customers are about their rational house feeling , such as comfortable living, environment and facility and house design decision, instead of income factor influences can change their earlier first house purchase decision if they feel the house price is more expensive to compare the other houses choices.

Second, the house developer can frame options differently by employing either an 'add' or 'delete' customization mode (or something in between). In an add mode, house buyers start with a base model and then add more or better options. In a delete frame, the opposite process occurs, whereby house buyers have to deselect options or downgrade from a fully-loaded model. Such as this house market case, past research suggests that house buyers end up choosing a greater number of features when they are in a delete rather than an add frame (Biswas, 2009). Finally, the option framing strategy will be associated with different house price anchors prior to customization, which may influence the perceived value of the house. If the final house ends up with one million house price bid, its cost is likely to be perceived as more attractive if the initial default configuration was two million house price (fully loaded) rather than one million house price. Why does the more expensive house price will still attract some house buyers to choose to buy in preference—an option framing strategy that maximizes sales, but set at a default house price that deters a minimum of potential house buyers from considering a purchase in the first place. When the house buyers group is high and stable income group, they won't consider the more expensive house price issue to influence them to change to buy the one million house price houses to live easily. Instead of after they view the house location to let them to feel that there have less transport facilities, e.g. bus, taxi, underground train, tram etc. public service transport tools are close to their living location, or tehy feel the natural environment is polluted to let they feel the can not breathe fresh air , or there are many factories are close to their houses to cause they feel dirty air, or traffic jam is serious to cause air pollution and noise pollution , or they feel that the two million house design is poor, they can not let them to feel comfortable to live in the appartments, it means that the house price is under value to be accepted to same to two million price. Then, the stable and high income house buyers will change their earlier house purchase first choice to accept the other house opitions to decide to buy in preference.

What is house buyer individual Rational Choice

In an ideal house market world, defaults, frames, and house price anchors would not have any bearing on consumer choices. House purchaser decisions would be the result of a careful weighing of costs and benefits and informed by existing preferences, such as whether the house future price will appreciate to raise value or reduce under value, the house living location will increase public transport facilities, public entertainment facilities, build more schools, offices to close to the house location. We would always make optimal decisions. In the 1976 book The Economic Approach to Human Behavior, the economist Gary S. Becker famously outlined a number of ideas known as the pillars of so-called 'rational choice' theory. The theory assumes that human actors have stable preferences and engage in maximizing behavior.

These psychological factors can influence housing buyer behaviors, they may include as below:

Mental Accounting influences housing buyer behavior

The economist Richard Thaler, a keen observer of human behavior and founder of behavioral economics, was inspired by Kahneman & Tversky's work (see Thaler, 2015, for a summary). Thaler coined the concept of mental accounting. According to Thaler, people think of value in relative rather than absolute terms. They derive pleasure not just from an object's value, but also the quality of the deal – its transaction utility (Thaler, 1985). In addition, humans often fail to fully consider opportunity costs (tradeoffs) and are susceptible to the sunk cost fallacy. Why are people willing to spend more when they pay with a credit card than cash (Prelec & Simester, 2001)? Why would more individuals spend $10 on a theater ticket if they had just lost a $10 bill than if they had to replace a lost ticket worth $10 (Kahneman & Tversky, 1984)? Why are people more likely to spend a small inheritance and invest a large one (Thaler, 1985)? Such as this property market case, if the house living needer , he/she does not choose to pay all money to buy the house, although he/she has enough money to buy the house. He/she chooses to pay instalement or rent the house to live. If he/she own visa card. Then, he/she will choose to use visa card to pay rent or pay month instalement to the property developer's house in order to earn accumulated money reward or any benefits after he/she use the visa to pay the house rent or instalement every month. So, the visa card can encourage the house buyer to achieve the house rent or instalement payment house purchase long term transaction easily.

According to the theory of mental accounting, people treat money differently, depending on factors such as the money's origin and intended use, rather than thinking of it in terms of the "bottom line" as in formal accounting (Thaler, 1999). An important term underlying the theory is fungibility, the fact that all money is interchangable and has no labels. In mental accounting, people treat assets as less fungible than they really are. Even seasoned investors are susceptible to this bias when they view recent gains as disposable "house money" (Thaler & Johnson, 1990) that can be used in high-risk investments. In doing so, they make decisions on each mental account separately, losing out the big picture of the portfolio.

Another concept related to mental accounting captures the fact that people don't like to spend money. We experience pain of paying (Zellermayer, 1996), because we are loss averse. The pain of paying plays an important role in consumer self-regulation to keep spending in check (Prelec & Loewenstein, 1998). This pain is thought to be reduced in credit card purchases, because plastic is less tangible than cash, the depletion of resources (money) is less visible and payment is deferred. Different types of people experience different levels of pain of paying, which can affect spending decisions. Tightwads, for instance, experience more of this pain than spendthrifts. As a result, tightwads are particularly sensitive to marketing contexts that make spending less painful (Rick, 2018). Hence, such as this property market purchase case, because some house buyers do not hope to spend much money to buy one house to live. They will feel to use visa card, it can replace money to let them to feel they won't lose much money to spend in the moment. So, in mental spending feeling view, they will feel visa card will help them to reduce to spend much money to rent or pay instalement to live the house in long time. So, in psychological view, visa card is one good spending money replace tool to influence these non- accepted spend money buyers to make final house rent or paying instalement decision to live the house decision more easily.

Choice Overload influences housing buyer behaviours

Humans' bounded rationality is particularly well illustrated by the concept of choice overload. Also referred to as 'overchoice', this phenomenon occurs as a result of too many choices being available to consumers. Overchoice has been associated with unhappiness (Schwartz, 2004), decision fatigue, going with the default option, as well as choice deferral—avoiding making a decision altogether, such as not buying a product (Iyengar & Lepper, 2000). Many different factors may contribute to perceived choice overload, including the number of options and attributes, time constraints, decision accountability, alignability and complementarity of options, consumers' preference uncertainty, among other factors (Chernev et al., 2015). Choice overload can be counteracted by simplifying choice attributes or the number of available options (Johnson et al., 2012). Hence, such as this property market case, when the month has too many properties are supplied to let house buyers to choose in the country's property market. Then, it will bring properties choice overload effect to cause the increasing houses number of options to cause the country's house buyers feel need to spend long time to make the house purchase preference decision in order to avoid any loss after they bought the under value houses to live. So, Choice overload usually cause long time choice process to any consumers, such as this property market consumption case.

Limited Information: The Importance of Feedback influences housing buyer behaviors

Bounded rationality's principle of limited knowledge or information is one of the topics discussed in the 2008 book Nudge. In the book, Thaler and Sunstein point to experience, good information, and prompt feedback as key factors that enable people to make good decisions. Consider climate change, for example, which has been cited as a particularly challenging problem in relation to experience and feedback. Climate change is invisible, diffuse, and a long-term process. Pro-environmental behavior by an individual, such as reducing carbon emissions, does not lead to a noticeable change. The same is true in the domain of health. Feedback in this area is often poor, and we are more likely to get feedback on previously chosen options than rejected ones.

Information Avoidance

Behavioral economics assumes that people are boundedly rational actors with a limited ability to process information. While a great deal of research has been devoted to exploring how available information affects the quality and outcomes of decisions, a newer strand of research has also explored situations where people avoid information altogether.

Information avoidance in behavioral economics (Golman et al., 2017) refers to situations in which people choose not to obtain knowledge that is freely available. Active information avoidance includes physical avoidance, inattention, the biased interpretation of information (see also confirmation bias) and even some forms of forgetting. In behavioral finance, for example, research has shown that investors are less likely to check their portfolio online when the stock market is down than when it is up, which has been termed the ostrich effect (Karlsson et al., 2009). More serious cases of avoidance happen when people fail to return to clinics to get medical test results, for instance (Sullivan et al., 2004).

While information avoidance is sometimes strategic, it can have immediate hedonic benefits for people if it prevents the negative (usually psychological) consequences of knowing the information. It usually carries negative utility in the long term, because it deprives people of potentially useful information for decision making and feedback for future behavior. Furthermore, information avoidance can contribute to a polarization of political opinions and media bias.

The impact of smoking, for example, is at best noticeable over the course of years, while its effect on cells and internal organs is usually not evident to the individual. Traditionally, generic feedback aimed at inducing behavioral change has been limited to information ranging from the economic costs of the unhealthy behavior to its potential health consequences (Diclemente et al., 2001). More recent behavior change programs, such as those employing smartphone apps to stop smoking, now usually provide positive and personalized behavioral feedback, which may include the number of cigarettes not smoked and money saved, along with information about health improvement and disease avoidance.

Predictably Irrational and Nudge alerted the public to a new breed of economists influenced by the study of behavioral decision making that was pioneered by Kahneman and Tversky's work (sometimes referred to as 'choice under uncertainty'). The psychology of homo economicus—a rational and selfish individual with relatively stable preferences—has been challenged, and the traditional view that behavior change should be achieved by informing, convincing, incentivizing or penalizing people has been questioned (Thaler & Sunstein, 2008). The field associated with this stream of research and theory is behavioral economics (BE), which suggests that human decisions are strongly influenced by context, including the way in which choices are presented to us. Behavior varies across time and space, and it is subject to cognitive biases, emotions, and social influences. Decisions are the result of less deliberative, linear, and controlled processes than we would like to believe.

Hence, such as this property market case, if the property developer can not provide more property advertisement to the property buyers to receive to let them to feel whether what benefits or enjoyment benefits that they can enjoy after they lived the property developer's houses to live. Due to lacking clear property information message to let many property buyers to know the property developer's property sale advertisement from property magazines, newspapers, TV, wesbite etc. channel. Then, it will influence the property developer's houses , they won't be many property buyers' choices, before they make final property purchase decision at the moment. So, property market purchase need desire change will be influenced by the time and space external unpredictable factor , such as visa card promotion , unemployment ratio rises up or falls down, the property advertisement attractive effort etc. unpredictable factors to excite any property buyers' living need desire in any time indirectly.

Dual-System Theory influences housing buyer behaviors

Daniel Kahneman uses a dual-system theoretical framework (which established a foothold in cognitive and social psychology of the 1990s) to explain why our judgments and decisions often do not conform to formal notions of rationality. System 1 consists of thinking processes that are intuitive, automatic, experience-based, and relatively unconscious. System 2 is more reflective, controlled, deliberative, and analytical. Judgments influenced by System 1 are rooted in impressions arising from mental content that is easily accessible. System 2, on the other hand, monitors or provides a check on mental operations and overt behavior—often unsuccessfully.

Example 1: Availability and Affect

System 1 is 'home' of the heuristics (cognitive shortcuts) we apply and responsible for the biases (systematic errors) we may be left with when we make decisions (Kahneman, 2011). System 1 processes influence us when prior exposure to a number affects subsequent judgments, as evident in the anchoring effects discussed previously (Tversky & Kahneman, 1974). One of the most universal heuristics is the availability heuristic. Availability serves as a mental shortcut if the possibility of an event occurring is perceived as higher simply because an example comes to mind easily

(Tversky & Kahneman, 1974); for instance, a person may deem pension investments too risky as a result of remembering a family member who lost most of her retirement savings in the recent recession. Readily available information in memory is also used when we make similarity-based judgments, as evident in the representativeness heuristic.

Finally, another 'general purpose' heuristic is that of affect, namely good or bad feelings that surface automatically when we think about an object. Applying the affect heuristic can lead to black-and-white thinking, which is particularly evident when people think about an object under conditions that hamper System 2 reflection, such as time pressure. For example, consumers may consider food preservatives' benefits as low and costs as high, thus leading to a significant negative risk-benefit correlation (Finucane, Alhakami, Slovic, & Johnson, 2000).

The role of affect in risky or uncertain situations is also evident in the risk-as-feelings model (Loewenstein, Weber, Hsee, & Welch, 2001). 'Consequentialist' accounts of decision making tend to focus on expectations along with the likelihood and desirability of possible outcomes. The risk-as-feelings perspective explains behavior in situations where emotional reactions to risk differ from cognitive evaluations. In these situations, behavior tends to be influenced by anticipatory feelings, emotions experienced in the moment of decision making.

Example 2: Salience

Availability and affect are processes internal to the individual that may lead to bias. The external equivalent of these processes is salience, whereby information that stands out, is novel, or seems relevant is more likely to affect our thinking and actions (Dolan et al., 2010). For example, a technological device can be framed as being 99% reliable or having only a 1% failure rate, thereby emphasizing either positive or negative information. Salience also underlies heuristic judgments that rely on external cues. Some psychologists have derived effort-reducing heuristics that simplify consumer decision making. The brand name heuristic, for example, suggests that salient cues in the form of brand names can be used to infer quality (Maheswaran, Mackie, & Chaiken, 1992). In terms of degrees of visual salience, one study found a congruence effect between price and font size, where showing a lower sale price in a small print size relative to the regular price resulted in greater purchase likelihood than presenting the sale price in a relatively large font (Coulter & Coulter, 2005). Finally, the salience of options can also be manipulated by rearranging the physical environment; for instance, a change as simple as moving water bottles closer to the cashier in a cafeteria has been shown to increase the salience and convenience of this healthier drink choice and thereby significantly boost water sales (Thorndike, Sonnenberg, Riis, Barraclough, & Levy, 2012).

Hence, such as this property market case, if the propety buyer feels that the property developer's house price won't be influenced to decrease easily in long time , even there are many property buyers still choose to buy the property developer's houses to live as well as the property developer's houses number supply won't increase in the long time. So, in Dual-System Theory explains if the house buyer felt that the property developer's house number supply won't increase, even decrease after there are many property buyers still chooce to buy its properties to live in preference in the country's property market. Then, the property developer's house high price and limited house supply factors will not influence the house buyer's prefer house choice decision more easily.

● How demand and supply view determines housing market buyer behaviors

How can demand and supply determine property market price ? Property price is arrived at by the interaction between house buyers demand and property developers' houses number supply. Property price is dependent upon the house design and environment and facilities characteristics of both these fundamental components of a property market. Any properties demand and supply represent the willingness of house consumers and property developers to engage in properties buyers buying needs or desires. An exchange of a house purchasetakes place when properties buyers and properties sellers can agree upon a agreed property price. This module will look at property price in a competitive market. When imperfect property market competition exists such as with a property developer monopoly or single peoperty selling firm, property price outcomes may not follow the same general rules.

Equilibrium Price in property market

When a property exchange occurs, the agreed upon price is called an "equilibrium" property price, or a "market clearing" price. This equilibrium property price occurs at the intersection of house demand and house supply as presented are in balance at the moment in property market short time, e.g. one month.

Property price determination depends equally on the moment house buyers' living demand and the moment house number supply. It is truly a balance of the two market components. To see why the balance must occur, examine what happens when there is no balance, for example when the moment property market price is below than the past property market price, the property quantity demanded is greater than the property quantity supplied. In such a situation, property consumers would be clamouring for a property that property developers would not be willing to supply; a property shortage would exist. In this event, property consumers would choose to pay a higher price in order to get the property they want, while property developers would be encouraged by a higher price to bring more of the properties onto the property market.

The end result is a rise in property price, when the moment has many proprety buyers feel living desire needs. where the property supply and demand are in balance. Similarly, if a property price is above were chosen arbitrarily the property market would be in shortage properties are supplied, too less properties supply are relative to high living desire demand. If that were to happen, properties developers would be willing to take a higher price in order to sell, and property consumers would be induced by higher prices to increase their property purchases desire , because they feel afraid that there will have less properties to be supplied to sell later and their prices will continue to raise in long time.

Hence, a property market price is not necessarily a fair price, it is merely an outcome. It does not guarantee total living satisfaction on the part of house buyer and property seller. Typically some assumptions about the behaviour of property buyers and property sellers are made, which add a sense of reason to a property market price. For example, property buyers are expected to be self-living comfortable interested and, although they may not have perfect property living and house price knowledge, at least they will try to look out for their own living interests. Meanwhile, property sellers are considered to be profit maximizers. This assumption limits their willingness to sell to within a price range , high to low, where they can stay in business.

Change in Equilibrium Price of property market

When either property demand or supply shifts, the property equilibrium price will change. Look at the modules on understanding property number supply for a discussion of why of that property market component may move. So, what factors can influence the property equilibrium price to be raise.

Example 1: Unusually environment and facility factor

When the property's location , it's environment and facilities are improved to let property buyers feel to compare before. With no immediate change in property consumers' willingness to buy the property developer's houses to live in the location at the moment because they feel that its environment and facilities can not let them to feel enough and comfortable to live in the location, there is a movement along the reducing demand curve to a new low equilibrium market price. Property consumers will buy more but only at a lower house price, becaue they feel poor environment and not enough facilities supply to influence they do not choose the property developer's houses location in preference. Otherwise, if the property demand curve in this example were more vertical (more inelastic, it means that the property developers raise their price won't influence less property buyers because their living desire is increasing), the property price-quantity adjustments needed to bring about a new equilibrium between property demand and the new property supply would be different. Then compare the size of property price-property quantity changes in this with the first situation. With the same shift in property supply, equilibrium change in property price is larger when property demand is inelastic than when property demand is more elastic. The opposite is true for property quantity. A larger change in property quantity supply will occur when property demand is elastic compared with the property quantity change required when property demand is inelastic.

How Does Property Developer Supply and House Buyer Demand Affect the Housing Market?

Real estate is a tangible asset made up of property and the land on which it sits. Like other assets, real estate is also subject to supply and demand. The prices of homes, like stocks and bonds, depend heavily on the law of supply and demand. But just what kind of relationship does the housing market have to this law? I suppose house supply number and house demad number , they must have close relationship to influence their house price changes in any time. Although, houses are expensive and fixed tangible asset, but they are still similar to general cheap product price changes to be influenced by demand and supply as below:

- The housing market relies very heavily on supply and demand.
- Housing demand and low supplies normally cause prices to rise.
- Prices drop when there is low demand and a larger supply of homes on the market.

•Low interest rates generally impact demand, while natural disasters, changing lifestyles, and the lack of available lots affect supplies.

The law of supply and demand is a basic economic principle that explains the relationship between supply and demand for a good or service, and how their interaction affects the price of that good or service. When there is high demand for a good or service, its price rises. If there is a large supply of a good or service but not enough demand for it, the price falls. The theory of supply and demand is one of the most basic principles in economics. Supply and demand work against each other until the point at which the equilibrium price is achieved—that is the price where supply is equal to demand in the market, such as property market case.

The law of demand dictates that people will have low or no demand for a good that has a higher price. That happens, of course, when all other factors remain equal. People tend to sacrifice something that comes at a higher cost, which curbs demand. Similarly, lower prices drive demand, meaning consumers value and purchase something more when it's cheaper. In fact, general property buyers' preference house purchase decision will be influenced by price factor in earlier. It is such as general cheap product demand and supply factor to influence its house price changes in any time. When it comes to the law of supply, prices drop when there is an increase in the supply of a good or service in the market. But when prices increase, the number of goods and services tend to drop. That's because it tends to cost more to produce and sell goods at a higher price.

Real Estate Supply and Demand

The housing market relies very heavily on supply and demand, which is why it is very prominent in the industry. Each housing transaction involves a buyer and a seller. The buyer places an offer on a property, leaving the seller to accept or reject the offer. The law of supply and demand dictates the equilibrium price of a property. Hence, supply and demand work against one another until the point at which a property's equilibrium price is reached.

A low property supply may drive prices up, which is what tends to happen with bidding wars. A specific property may be in demand by multiple parties who try to outbid each other by increasing their purchase price offer. The bidding war ends—depleting the supply—when the seller accepts one of the offers. When there is high demand for properties in a particular city or state, and a lack of supply of quality properties, the prices of houses tend to rise. When a weak economy and an oversupply of properties leads to low or no demand for housing, the prices of houses tend to fall.

Factors Affecting Housing Supply and Demand

Supply and demand is never an easy thing to measure in the real estate market. That's partly due because it takes a long time to construct new homes and fix up old ones to put back onto the market. Similarly, real estate is not like other industries in that it takes a lot of time to buy and sell homes and other properties. Some of the factors that influence housing demand include lower interest rates or borrowing costs in economic environment view. When interest rates are low, people are generally willing to take on more debt. They may be able to finance the purchase of a home because the amount of interest they have to pay isn't burdensome. If more buyers flood the market, demand for housing increases. And if there's a limited supply of housing inventory, that makes people in a low interest rate environment want to purchase even more.

Meanwhile, the supply of housing is in a constant state of change. Inventory may increase when people are moving—some may downsize, others may be try to make more room for an expanding family, while others may purchase their first home. Similarly, there may be an increase in development and new home construction, adding to the existing inventory. On the other hand, housing inventory decreases during times of natural disaster—such as floods and earthquakes—and when existing properties are demolished. Land is also a finite resource, so the amount of new developments is generally limited. It is unpredicted environmental factor to influence property price changes in the moment.

Economic environment factor influences property price changes

One of the major causes of the Great Recession that followed the financial crisis in the mid-2000s was the housing market crash. It was a direct result of the law of supply and demand. During the lead up to the financial crisis, consumers were enjoying relatively low borrowing rates. Banks began to offer low rates on mortgages, and were encouraged to relax their lending standards. People who weren't otherwise able to afford a home now found themselves able to realize their dreams. These consumers, called subprime borrowers, were able to snag a home with low down payments and low credit scores.

During this time, speculative buyers also began entering the market, driving up demand for housing and, at the same time, cutting in to the available supply. All of this, in turn, drove prices up to very lofty levels. The market couldn't keep up, and investors who were merely in the market to make some money—many were buying and flipping homes in a very short period of time—began pulling out of the market. Demand started to drop and, so did prices. The collapse of the real estate market in 2007 created an oversupply of houses and decreasing properties prices. Real estate prices depend on the law of supply and demand. When the demand for property is high but property is scarce, prices skyrocket and it becomes a seller's market. When the number of available properties increases to glut the market, prices typically drop. Supply and demand in real estate aren't easy to balance. Creating more saleable properties takes time, considerable work, and a lot of effort. It's not possible at all in some cases, and even when it is, it might not be possible for supply to increase in time to meet consumer demand. So, salespeoples‘ house sale experiences can also influence the property developer's house sale number.

Understanding this basic economic principle can help consumers decide the best time to buy or sell their properties.

Property market Over-Supply Or Under-Supply factor

You can usually expect a drop in prices when there is an over-supply of homes or land in a given area. You can't move the overage to another area to keep prices stable. Scarcity causes prices to rise when there isn't enough land or if there aren't enough homes in a given area. Even if land is available on which to build more homes, the time it takes to construct them cannot meet immediate property needs, so demand will remain constant or rise. Many forces that might have little or no impact on other regions influence local markets and vice versa. Pay attention to the factors that influence your local market. Watch local businesses and make note of upsizing and downsizing trends if you do business in a market that has jobs and many workers relocating there. You'll also want to keep an eye on these issues if you're a homeowner looking to sell in such an area or if you're looking for property to purchase.

Things like divorce rates, death rates, and demographics can factor in. Factors that can greatly impact property market supply and demand—and by extension your business—might include local weather trends, an aging population, and investment trends if you do business in a resort area that includes vacation homes. Trends that impact discretionary income have more of an influence on this type of market than others. Trends in interest rates, national home prices, new housing starts, and many other economic indicators can influence real estate markets as well. These national events might not typically move real estate supply and demand directly, but they can render it less or more important. The mood and sentiments of the buying public cannot be overlooked. Supply and demand don't exist in a vacuum. But few could afford to pay those prices in a worsening economy and even those who could were understandably reluctant to part with their money at that time. So properties sat on the market, unsold. Worried homeowners in financial distress put their homes up for sale rather than risk foreclosure. Remember, almost 9 million jobs were lost during the Great Recession. Now what happens? Supply begins surpassing demand by leaps and bounds. The housing market is glutted and those healthy prices evaporate—which has little to do with local factors except as they're an extension of national woes.

Land Parcels Are Finite factor to influence property market price

If the country has high population, but land supply is less to let property developers to find lands to build houses easily. Such as Hong Kong is one high population and small city. So, its property prices must be higher to compare other countries, and it causes that its rooms and houses size or area is small , but house sale price or rent is still high.

Such as Hong Kong house market case, Hong Kong people cannot fill a real estate supply shortage by manufacturing more units of land. It's a finite supply, not a manufactured commodity. Hong Kong people might be able to create more units within a given space, such as condos or townhouses, but the land itself is unique and cannot be duplicated to accommodate a short supply. When a shortage of land for homes exists in a given area, Hong Kong people can't simply move in more land to alleviate the shortage. Real estate is where it sits. It will always be a local commodity influenced by local conditions. In short, keep up with the big picture but narrow your primary focus to your region. Supply and demand in real estate will always be foremost a local issue.

As with many other types of business market, the property market is driven by supply and demand. Property prices fluctuate depending upon the factors that influence both supply and demand. Knowledge of these factors equips you with the capability of knowing when to rent/buy and, perhaps just as importantly, when to sell. At the most basic level, when property supply is greater than demand, prices fall. That's the nature of almost every product. Similarly, when the demand for properties is greater than the available supply, prices rise. Even though property markets have these principles in common with many other types of products or business services, there are some differences worth mentioning. For example, the real estate market also takes into consideration factors such as location, seasonality, and durability. There are also different types of real estate – residential, industrial, commercial and land – each of which has their own factors that influence market supply and demand. "Real estate" is defined as more than just property. It also includes natural resources and land, too. So, Hong Kong property market's price is influenced by land supply factor more than other factors, such as facilities , environment , transport etc. factors influence.

Local factors that influence property rates include:

1 – Restrictions on property production – for instance, in the case of Manhatten, there is not much space for added supply. As a result, demand remains high and prices even higher.

2 – Credit access – this often depends on where individuals live. Rural communities may have less access to bank credit, for example – reducing demand.

3 – Job market – the more jobs, the greater the demand for properties.

4 – Transport – better transport translates into greater desirability for people to move – increasing demand.

5 – Retired persons – retired people often decide to downsize and opt for a smaller property in a different locality, thereby increasing supply.

6 – Families – as families begin to grow, they need greater sized properties. This increases the demand for larger homes, whilst decreasing demand for smaller homes.

7 – Meteorology – destinations with more favorable weather profiles and ones that avert the extremes of weather are preferable. Demand in places such as San Diego is significantly higher than the tornado alleys of Alabama.

8 – Income – if income levels in a locality are generally high, there is more money in the market to purchase homes, decreasing supply and increasing prices.

9 – Construction market – the greater the degree of construction of new properties, the greater the supply in the market.

Understanding the factors that drive market supply and demand, and hence property prices are important. The more informed about these nine factors, the better purchasing/selling decisions you can make. For example – designs and styles and fads come and go into "fashion", and what design/

style/fad factors elevate a property price one-year can diminish the price of a property the following year. If you are managing a property, you can factor these decisions when determining optimum rent or a selling value.

When borrowing rates are lower, properties become more affordable. This, too, influences demand. Tax credits, for example – for first-time buyers – can encourage more buyers to seek interest in the property market. As well as this, there are various social factors involved, too – such as the social status afforded to people who own their own homes. Age can come into play here, too, depending on the city and what social expectations young professionals have.

What drives property market supply and demand, then, is an interweaving network of factors, many of which playoff on one another. It's important to appreciate the impact that each of these individual factors has and how they influence property prices throughout the country.

How to Analyze Supply and Demand For Apartment Buildings

One of the most important ways to use all of the data gathered in a real estate market analysis is to examine the supply and demand factors for a particular type of real estate. For example, an investor considering the construction or purchase of a new multifamily residential property uses the market analysis to determine what cash flows they can expect to receive given the expected demand for units. The demand must be high enough to generate cash flows that provide a rate of return high enough to make the investment feasible.

In order to estimate the demand for multifamily housing units, it is necessary to understand recent population growth trends for the city. Then, it's important to consider the major industries in the market area and the forecasted growth for those industries over the next few years. You can then put this information together to forecast multifamily housing demand and compare that demand to the existing and proposed supply of multifamily units. This case study takes data about population and industrial activity in the Orlando, Florida region and analyzes supply and demand of multifamily residential units in the region.

Population Trends and Apartment Building Demand

Recent data from the U.S. Census Bureau and the Orlando Economic Development Commission lists the total population of the Orlando metro area at 2,387,138 (2016). Between 2015 and 2016, the population of the Orlando metro area grew by 2.6%. That made Orlando the fastest growing region in the United States. The Orlando Economic Development

Commission estimates that population growth in the region since 2000 equates to a gain of 138 people per day. Population growth is mostly fueled by domestic migration. Americans moving to Orlando for retirement in warmer weather or for new career opportunities account for about 40% of the population increase. International migration (mainly from Central and South America) accounts for 34% of the increase in population. People have been moving to the Orlando area due to the region's comparative advantages (climate, entertainment and lifestyle, and economic growth). Without these advantages, Orlando would not be one of the fastest growing regions of the country.

With an average household size around 2.5, that means there are an estimated 954,855 households in the Orlando metropolitan area. Data from the American Consumer Survey indicates that about 43% of the population is renters. So, 43% of households would give an estimated demand of 410,588 multifamily units. In reality, not all renters live in multifamily units since many rent single-family homes. Therefore, it is necessary to estimate how many of those renters occupy multifamily units. A 2016 report from Fannie Mae estimated that there were 156,000 multifamily units in the Orlando metro area with a 5.75% vacancy rate. So, in 2016 there were around 147,030 occupied multifamily units (156,000 x (1-.0575) = 147,030). This means an estimated 35.8% of the households that are renters occupy multifamily units while the remaining 64.2% of renters occupy single-family homes.

Economic Trends and Multifamily Housing Demand

Employment data from the Bureau of Labor Statistics confirms that economic growth is driving the population growth in the Orlando metro area. In fact, job growth from 2015-2016 in Orlando was over twice the national average. A strong economy and growth in the number of jobs indicates that the population should continue to grow over the next few years unless there is a major shift to the national economy or a natural disaster. Furthermore, the job growth rate of 4.22% exceeded the population growth rate of 2.6%. If the major industries in Orlando continue to grow at this pace, more new workers will need to move into the region to fill these new jobs. So, forecasted population growth may be higher than the average of 2% seen over the past 10 years. It might be more appropriate to estimate population growth of at least 3% annually.

As with commodities traded on the market, housing prices continually fluctuate, sometimes with drastic changes over a short period of time.

Availability is a huge factor affecting prices within a set region, such as in a specific suburb of a metropolitan area. Likewise, demand for homes in that market also plays into that price, which is why two nearly identical homes in different cities may sell for vastly different prices. When buying a home in a seller's market, limit your contingencies and make your offer as favorable to the seller as possible.

For houses and virtually anything else available for purchase, supply and demand play into the ultimate selling price. When an item is in short supply and many people want it, prices tend to rise. When the market is flooded with an item or there's no demand for it, prices fall. Sporting event ticket prices tend to rise when a team reaches the championship level, yet tickets to the same team's events a few years later, when the team isn't doing well, cost far less. Prices on holiday decor are another great example: At the peak of any holiday's shopping season, some shoppers are willing to pay a premium for the decor. Three days after the holiday, the leftover stock of these items is marked down to clearance prices due to little demand.

Housing supply and demand works in exactly the same way. Sometimes there are so many single-family homes available in the same region that there aren't enough buyers for all of them. In this housing oversupply, prices drop to draw more attention from potential buyers. A lowered price may influence an interested buyer to choose one home over a similar house in the same general area. Without a lowered price, a house may sit on the market for months due to the abundant number of similar homes for sale nearby at the same time.

On conclusion, property price change can be influenced by house buyers living need and land and house number supply factor, but any house buyer individual rational will influence his/her prerference property choice decision before he / she decides to choose what kinds properties or anywhere locations to live. So, house buyer individual psychological factor will influence his/her properties choices.

Behavioral economy predicts
house buyers purchase living desire

Can internet influence property buyers' house locations, prices and property developers choices changes ? How and why behavioral economic method can predict house buyers house purchase need or desire whether the country's house buyers their house purchase need or desire will increase or decrease in the year. I shall explain the reasons as below:

What does behavioral economy mean ?Think about supposing you plan to buy a house. You may have decided to simplify your decision making by opting for the house price, living environment, such as air and noise pollution, income level, school, public library, public park, public swimming pool, transportation facilities etc. different factors to influence you house purchase decision in the location. You may then have visited the house location to view its environments before you decide to choose the location to buy the house to live. But the decision making process did not stop there, as you now had to customize your model by visiting from different house location . You aim to compare whether anywhere location(s) can let you to feel the location is better to let you feel to live.) Instead the house location and environment factor, you were still considered the house appearance and design and comfortable feeling features you really needed. At this stage, most property developers will show a base model with options that can be changed according to whether the house buyers their preferences are environment, house design, house price, facilties before they decide to buy the house to live. The way in which these different location of house choices are presented to house buyers will influence the final house purchases made and illustrates a number of concepts from behavioral economic (BE) theories.

First, the base model shown in the customization engine represents a rational choice to any house buyers‘ purchase decision usually. Usually, house buyers, they will visit the house location to feel its living environment, entertainment facilities supply, transport facilities supply and house design and comfortable feeling to decide to buy the house to live, instead of income factor in house market. The more uncertain house customers are about their rational house feeling , such as comfortable living, environment and facility and house design decision, instead of income factor influences can change their earlier first house purchase decision if they feel the house price is more expensive to compare the other houses choices.

Second, the house developer can frame options differently by employing either an 'add' or 'delete' customization mode (or something in between). In an add mode, house buyers start with a base model and then add more or better options. In a delete frame, the opposite process occurs, whereby house buyers have to deselect options or downgrade from a fully-loaded model. Such as this house market case, past research suggests that house buyers end up choosing a greater number of features when they are in a delete rather than an add frame (Biswas, 2009). Finally, the option framing strategy will be associated with different house price anchors prior to customization, which may influence the perceived value of the house. If the final house ends up with one million house price bid, its cost is likely to be perceived as more attractive if the initial default configuration was two million house price (fully loaded) rather than one million house price. Why does the more expensive house price will still attract some house buyers to choose to buy in preference—an option framing strategy that maximizes sales, but set at a default house price that deters a minimum of potential house buyers from considering a purchase in the first place. When the house buyers group is high and stable income group, they won't consider the more expensive house price issue to influence them to change to buy the one million house price houses to live easily. Instead of after they view the house location to let them to feel that there have less transport facilities, e.g. bus, taxi, underground train, tram etc. public service transport tools are close to their living location, or tehy feel the natural environment is polluted to let they feel the can not breathe fresh air , or there are many factories are close to their houses to cause they feel dirty air, or traffic jam is serious to cause air pollution and noise pollution , or they feel that the two million house design is poor, they can not let them to feel comfortable to live in the appartments, it means that the house price is under value to be accepted to same to two million price. Then, the stable and high income house buyers will change their earlier house purchase first choice to accept the other house opitions to decide to buy in preference.

What is house buyer individual Rational Choice

In an ideal house market world, defaults, frames, and house price anchors would not have any bearing on consumer choices. House purchaser decisions would be the result of a careful weighing of costs and benefits and informed by existing preferences, such as whether the house future price will appreciate to raise value or reduce under value, the house living location will increase public transport facilities, public entertainment facilities, build more schools, offices to close to the house location. We would always make optimal decisions. In the 1976 book The Economic Approach to Human Behavior, the economist Gary S. Becker famously outlined a number of ideas known as the pillars of so-called 'rational choice' theory. The theory assumes that human actors have stable preferences and engage in maximizing behavior.

Mental Accounting

The economist Richard Thaler, a keen observer of human behavior and founder of behavioral economics, was inspired by Kahneman & Tversky's work (see Thaler, 2015, for a summary). Thaler coined the concept of mental accounting. According to Thaler, people think of value in relative rather than absolute terms. They derive pleasure not just from an object's value, but also the quality of the deal – its transaction utility (Thaler, 1985). In addition, humans often fail to fully consider opportunity costs (tradeoffs) and are susceptible to the sunk cost fallacy. Why are people willing to spend more when they pay with a credit card than cash (Prelec & Simester, 2001)? Why would more individuals spend $10 on a theater ticket if they had just lost a $10 bill than if they had to replace a lost ticket worth $10 (Kahneman & Tversky, 1984)? Why are people more likely to spend a small inheritance and invest a large one (Thaler, 1985)? Such as this property market case, if the house living needer , he/she does not choose to pay all money to buy the house, although he/she has enough money to buy the house. He/she chooses to pay instalement or rent the house to live. If he/she own visa card. Then, he/she will choose to use visa card to pay rent or pay month instalement to the property developer's house in order to earn accumulated money reward or any benefits after he/she use the visa to pay the house rent or instalement every month. So, the visa card can encourage the house buyer to achieve the house rent or instalement payment house purchase long term transaction easily.

According to the theory of mental accounting, people treat money differently, depending on factors such as the money's origin and intended use, rather than thinking of it in terms of the "bottom line" as in formal accounting (Thaler, 1999). An important term underlying the theory is fungibility, the fact that all money is interchangable and has no labels. In mental accounting, people treat assets as less fungible than they really are. Even seasoned investors are susceptible to this bias when they view recent gains as disposable "house money" (Thaler & Johnson, 1990) that can be used in high-risk investments. In doing so, they make decisions on each mental account separately, losing out the big picture of the portfolio.

Another concept related to mental accounting captures the fact that people don't like to spend money. We experience pain of paying (Zellermayer, 1996), because we are loss averse. The pain of paying plays an important role in consumer self-regulation to keep spending in check (Prelec &

Loewenstein, 1998). This pain is thought to be reduced in credit card purchases, because plastic is less tangible than cash, the depletion of resources (money) is less visible and payment is deferred. Different types of people experience different levels of pain of paying, which can affect spending decisions. Tightwads, for instance, experience more of this pain than spendthrifts. As a result, tightwads are particularly sensitive to marketing contexts that make spending less painful (Rick, 2018). Hence, such as this property market purchase case, because some house buyers do not hope to spend much money to buy one house to live. They will feel to use visa card, it can replace money to let them to feel they won't lose much money to spend in the moment. So, in mental spending feeling view, they will feel visa card will help them to reduce to spend much money to rent or pay instalement to live the house in long time. So, in psychological view, visa card is one good spending money replace tool to influence these non- accepted spend money buyers to make final house rent or paying instalement decision to live the house decision more easily.

Choice Overload

Humans' bounded rationality is particularly well illustrated by the concept of choice overload. Also referred to as 'overchoice', this phenomenon occurs as a result of too many choices being available to consumers. Overchoice has been associated with unhappiness (Schwartz, 2004), decision fatigue, going with the default option, as well as choice deferral—avoiding making a decision altogether, such as not buying a product (Iyengar & Lepper, 2000). Many different factors may contribute to perceived choice overload, including the number of options and attributes, time constraints, decision accountability, alignability and complementarity of options, consumers' preference uncertainty, among other factors (Chernev et al., 2015). Choice overload can be counteracted by simplifying choice attributes or the number of available options (Johnson et al., 2012). Hence, such as this property market case, when the month has too many properties are supplied to let house buyers to choose in the country's property market. Then, it will bring properties choice overload effect to cause the increasing houses number of options to cause the country's house buyers feel need to spend long time to make the house purchase preference decision in order to avoid any loss after they bought the under value houses to live. So, Choice overload usually cause long time choice process to any consumers, such as this property market consumption case.

Limited Information: The Importance of Feedback

Bounded rationality's principle of limited knowledge or information is one of the topics discussed in the 2008 book Nudge. In the book, Thaler and Sunstein point to experience, good information, and prompt feedback as key factors that enable people to make good decisions. Consider climate change, for example, which has been cited as a particularly challenging problem in relation to experience and feedback. Climate change is invisible, diffuse, and a long-term process. Pro-environmental behavior by an individual, such as reducing carbon emissions, does not lead to a noticeable change. The same is true in the domain of health. Feedback in this area is often poor, and we are more likely to get feedback on previously chosen options than rejected ones.

Information Avoidance

Behavioral economics assumes that people are boundedly rational actors with a limited ability to process information. While a great deal of research has been devoted to exploring how available information affects the quality and outcomes of decisions, a newer strand of research has also explored situations where people avoid information altogether.

Information avoidance in behavioral economics (Golman et al., 2017) refers to situations in which people choose not to obtain knowledge that is freely available. Active information avoidance includes physical avoidance, inattention, the biased interpretation of information (see also confirmation bias) and even some forms of forgetting. In behavioral finance, for example, research has shown that investors are less likely to check their portfolio online when the stock market is down than when it is up, which has been termed the ostrich effect (Karlsson et al., 2009). More serious cases of avoidance happen when people fail to return to clinics to get medical test results, for instance (Sullivan et al., 2004).

While information avoidance is sometimes strategic, it can have immediate hedonic benefits for people if it prevents the negative (usually psychological) consequences of knowing the information. It usually carries negative utility in the long term, because it deprives people of potentially useful information for decision making and feedback for future behavior. Furthermore, information avoidance can contribute to a polarization of political opinions and media bias.

The impact of smoking, for example, is at best noticeable over the course of years, while its effect on cells and internal organs is usually not evident to the individual. Traditionally, generic feedback aimed at inducing behavioral change has been limited to information ranging from the economic costs of the unhealthy behavior to its potential health consequences (Diclemente et al., 2001). More recent behavior change programs, such as those employing smartphone apps to stop smoking, now usually provide positive and personalized behavioral feedback, which may include the number of cigarettes not smoked and money saved, along with information about health improvement and disease avoidance.

Predictably Irrational and Nudge alerted the public to a new breed of economists influenced by the study of behavioral decision making that was pioneered by Kahneman and Tversky's work (sometimes referred to as 'choice under uncertainty'). The psychology of homo economicus—a rational and selfish individual with relatively stable preferences—has been challenged, and the traditional view that behavior change should be achieved by informing, convincing, incentivizing or penalizing people has been questioned (Thaler & Sunstein, 2008). The field associated with this stream of research and theory is behavioral economics (BE), which suggests that human decisions are strongly influenced by context, including the way in which choices are presented to us. Behavior varies across time and space, and it is subject to cognitive biases, emotions, and social influences. Decisions are the result of less deliberative, linear, and controlled processes than we would like to believe.

Hence, such as this property market case, if the property developer can not provide more property advertisement to the property buyers to receive to let them to feel whether what benefits or enjoyment benefits that they can enjoy after they lived the property developer's houses to live. Due to lacking clear property information message to let many property buyers to know the property developer's property sale advertisement from property magazines, newspapers, TV, wesbite etc. channel. Then, it will influence the property developer's houses , they won't be many property buyers' choices, before they make final property purchase decision at the moment. So, property market purchase need desire change will be influenced by the time and space external unpredictable factor , such as visa card promotion , unemployment ratio rises up or falls down, the property advertisement attractive effort etc. unpredictable factors to excite any property buyers' living need desire in any time indirectly.

Dual-System Theory

Daniel Kahneman uses a dual-system theoretical framework (which established a foothold in cognitive and social psychology of the 1990s) to explain why our judgments and decisions often do not conform to formal notions of rationality. System 1 consists of thinking processes that are intuitive, automatic, experience-based, and relatively unconscious. System 2 is more reflective, controlled, deliberative, and analytical. Judgments influenced by System 1 are rooted in impressions arising from mental content that is easily accessible. System 2, on the other hand, monitors or provides a check on mental operations and overt behavior—often unsuccessfully.

Example 1: Availability and Affect

System 1 is 'home' of the heuristics (cognitive shortcuts) we apply and responsible for the biases (systematic errors) we may be left with when we make decisions (Kahneman, 2011). System 1 processes influence us when prior exposure to a number affects subsequent judgments, as evident in the anchoring effects discussed previously (Tversky & Kahneman, 1974). One of the most universal heuristics is the availability heuristic. Availability serves as a mental shortcut if the possibility of an event occurring is perceived as higher simply because an example comes to mind easily (Tversky & Kahneman, 1974); for instance, a person may deem pension investments too risky as a result of remembering a family member who lost most of her retirement savings in the recent recession. Readily available information in memory is also used when we make similarity-based judgments, as evident in the representativeness heuristic.

Finally, another 'general purpose' heuristic is that of affect, namely good or bad feelings that surface automatically when we think about an object. Applying the affect heuristic can lead to black-and-white thinking, which is particularly evident when people think about an object under conditions that hamper System 2 reflection, such as time pressure. For example, consumers may consider food preservatives' benefits as low and costs as high, thus leading to a significant negative risk-benefit correlation (Finucane, Alhakami, Slovic, & Johnson, 2000).

The role of affect in risky or uncertain situations is also evident in the risk-as-feelings model (Loewenstein, Weber, Hsee, & Welch, 2001). 'Consequentialist' accounts of decision making tend to focus on expectations along with the likelihood and desirability of possible outcomes. The risk-as-feelings perspective explains behavior in situations where emotional reactions to risk differ from cognitive evaluations. In these situations, behavior tends to be influenced by anticipatory feelings, emotions experienced in the moment of decision making.

Example 2: Salience

Availability and affect are processes internal to the individual that may lead to bias. The external equivalent of these processes is salience, whereby information that stands out, is novel, or seems relevant is more likely to affect our thinking and actions (Dolan et al., 2010). For example, a technological device can be framed as being 99% reliable or having only a 1% failure rate, thereby emphasizing either positive or negative information. Salience also underlies heuristic judgments that rely on external cues. Some psychologists have derived effort-reducing heuristics that simplify consumer decision making. The brand name heuristic, for example, suggests that salient cues in the form of brand names can be used to infer quality (Maheswaran, Mackie, & Chaiken, 1992). In terms of degrees of visual salience, one study found a congruence effect between price and font size, where showing a lower sale price in a small print size relative to the regular price resulted in greater purchase likelihood than presenting the sale price in a relatively large font (Coulter & Coulter, 2005). Finally, the salience of options can also be manipulated by rearranging the physical environment; for instance, a change as simple as moving water bottles closer to the cashier in a cafeteria has been shown to increase the salience and convenience of this healthier drink choice and thereby significantly boost water sales (Thorndike, Sonnenberg, Riis, Barraclough, & Levy, 2012).

Hence, such as this property market case, if the propety buyer feels that the property developer's house price won't be influenced to decrease easily in long time , even there are many property buyers still choose to buy the property developer's houses to live as well as the property developer's houses number supply won't increase in the long time. So, in Dual-System Theory explains if the house buyer felt that the property developer's house number supply won't increase, even decrease after there are many property buyers still chooce to buy its properties to live in preference in the country's property market. Then, the property developer's house high price and limited house supply factors will not influence the house buyer's prefer house choice decision more easily.

● Internet influences property market demand and supply view

How can demand and supply determine property market price ? Property price is arrived at by the interaction between house buyers demand and property developers' houses number supply. Property price is dependent upon the house design and environment and facilities characteristics of both these fundamental components of a property market. Any properties demand and supply represent the willingness of house consumers and property developers to engage in properties buyers buying needs or desires. An exchange of a house purchasetakes place when properties buyers and properties sellers can agree upon a agreed property price. This module will look at property price in a competitive market. When imperfect property market competition exists such as with a property developer monopoly or single peoperty selling firm, property price outcomes may not follow the same general rules.

Equilibrium Price in property market

When a property exchange occurs, the agreed upon price is called an "equilibrium" property price, or a "market clearing" price. This equilibrium property price occurs at the intersection of house demand and house supply as presented are in balance at the moment in property market short time, e.g. one month.

Property price determination depends equally on the moment house buyers‘ living demand and the moment house number supply. It is truly a balance of the two market components. To see why the balance must occur, examine what happens when there is no balance, for example when the moment property market price is below than the past property market price, the property quantity demanded is greater than the property quantity supplied. In such a situation, property consumers would be clamouring for a property that property developers would not be willing to supply; a property shortage would exist. In this event, property consumers would choose to pay a higher price in order to get the property they want, while property developers would be encouraged by a higher price to bring more of the properties onto the property market.

The end result is a rise in property price, when the moment has many proprety buyers feel living desire needs. where the property supply and demand are in balance. Similarly, if a property price is above were chosen arbitrarily the property market would be in shortage properties are supplied, too less properties supply are relative to high living desire demand. If that were to happen, properties developers would be willing to take a higher price in order to sell, and property consumers would be induced by higher prices to increase their property purchases desire , because they feel afraid that there will have less properties to be supplied to sell later and their prices will continue to raise in long time.

Hence, a property market price is not necessarily a fair price, it is merely an outcome. It does not guarantee total living satisfaction on the part of house buyer and property seller. Typically some assumptions about the behaviour of property buyers and property sellers are made, which add a sense of reason to a property market price. For example, property buyers are expected to be self-living comfortable interested and, although they may not have perfect property living and house price knowledge, at least they will try to look out for their own living interests. Meanwhile, property sellers are considered to be profit maximizers. This assumption limits their willingness to sell to within a price range , high to low, where they can stay in business.

Change in Equilibrium Price of property market

When either property demand or supply shifts, the property equilibrium price will change. Look at the modules on understanding property number supply for a discussion of why of that property market component may move. So, what factors can influence the property equilibrium price to be raise.

Example 1: Unusually environment and facility factor

When the property's location , it's environment and facilities are improved to let property buyers feel to compare before. With no immediate change in property consumers' willingness to buy the property developer's houses to live in the location at the moment because they feel that its environment and facilities can not let them to feel enough and comfortable to live in the location, there is a movement along the reducing demand curve to a new low equilibrium market price. Property consumers will buy more but only at a lower house price, becaue they feel poor environment and not enough facilities supply to influence they do not choose the property developer's houses location in preference. Otherwise, if the property demand curve in this example were more vertical (more inelastic, it means that the property developers raise their price won't influence less property buyers because their living desire is increasing), the property price-quantity adjustments needed to bring about a new equilibrium between property demand and the new property supply would be different. Then compare the size of property price-property quantity changes in this with the first situation. With the same shift in property supply, equilibrium change in property price is larger when property demand is inelastic than when property demand is more elastic. The opposite is true for property quantity. A larger change in property quantity supply will occur when property demand is elastic compared with the property quantity change required when property demand is inelastic.

How Does Property Developer Supply and House Buyer Demand Affect the Housing Market?

Real estate is a tangible asset made up of property and the land on which it sits. Like other assets, real estate is also subject to supply and demand. The prices of homes, like stocks and bonds, depend heavily on the law of supply and demand. But just what kind of relationship does the housing market have to this law? I suppose house supply number and house demad number , they must have close relationship to influence their house price changes in any time. Although, houses are expensive and fixed tangible asset, but they are still similar to general cheap product price changes to be influenced by demand and supply as below:

•The housing market relies very heavily on supply and demand.

•Housing demand and low supplies normally cause prices to rise.

•Prices drop when there is low demand and a larger supply of homes on the market.

•Low interest rates generally impact demand, while natural disasters, changing lifestyles, and the lack of available lots affect supplies.

The law of supply and demand is a basic economic principle that explains the relationship between supply and demand for a good or service, and how their interaction affects the price of that good or service. When there is high demand for a good or service, its price rises. If there is a large supply of a good or service but not enough demand for it, the price falls. The theory of supply and demand is one of the most basic principles in economics. Supply and demand work against each other until the point at which the equilibrium price is achieved—that is the price where supply is equal to demand in the market, such as property market case.

The law of demand dictates that people will have low or no demand for a good that has a higher price. That happens, of course, when all other factors remain equal. People tend to sacrifice something that comes at a higher cost, which curbs demand. Similarly, lower prices drive demand, meaning consumers value and purchase something more when it's cheaper. In fact, general property buyers' preference house purchase decision will be influenced by price factor in earlier. It is such as general cheap product demand and supply factor to influence its house price changes in any time.

When it comes to the law of supply, prices drop when there is an increase in the supply of a good or service in the market. But when prices increase, the number of goods and services tend to drop. That's because it tends to cost more to produce and sell goods at a higher price.

Real Estate Supply and Demand

The housing market relies very heavily on supply and demand, which is why it is very prominent in the industry. Each housing transaction involves a buyer and a seller. The buyer places an offer on a property, leaving the seller to accept or reject the offer. The law of supply and demand dictates the equilibrium price of a property. Hence, supply and demand work against one another until the point at which a property's equilibrium price is reached.

A low property supply may drive prices up, which is what tends to happen with bidding wars. A specific property may be in demand by multiple parties who try to outbid each other by increasing their purchase price offer. The bidding war ends—depleting the supply—when the seller accepts one of the offers. When there is high demand for properties in a particular city or state, and a lack of supply of quality properties, the prices of houses tend to rise. When a weak economy and an oversupply of properties leads to low or no demand for housing, the prices of houses tend to fall.

Factors Affecting Housing Supply and Demand

Supply and demand is never an easy thing to measure in the real estate market. That's partly due because it takes a long time to construct new homes and fix up old ones to put back onto the market. Similarly, real estate is not like other industries in that it takes a lot of time to buy and sell homes and other properties. Some of the factors that influence housing demand include lower interest rates or borrowing costs in economic environment view. When interest rates are low, people are generally willing to take on more debt. They may be able to finance the purchase of a home because the amount of interest they have to pay isn't burdensome. If more buyers flood the market, demand for housing increases. And if there's a limited supply of housing inventory, that makes people in a low interest rate environment want to purchase even more.

Meanwhile, the supply of housing is in a constant state of change. Inventory may increase when people are moving—some may downsize, others may be try to make more room for an expanding family, while others may purchase their first home. Similarly, there may be an increase in development and new home construction, adding to the existing inventory. On the other hand, housing inventory decreases during times of natural disaster—such as floods and earthquakes—and when existing properties are demolished. Land is also a finite resource, so the amount of new developments is generally limited. It is unpredicted environmental factor to influence property price changes in the moment.

Economic environment factor influences property price changes

One of the major causes of the Great Recession that followed the financial crisis in the mid-2000s was the housing market crash. It was a direct result of the law of supply and demand. During the lead up to the financial crisis, consumers were enjoying relatively low borrowing rates. Banks began to offer low rates on mortgages, and were encouraged to relax their lending standards. People who weren't otherwise able to afford a home now found themselves able to realize their dreams. These consumers, called subprime borrowers, were able to snag a home with low down payments and low credit scores.

During this time, speculative buyers also began entering the market, driving up demand for housing and, at the same time, cutting in to the available supply. All of this, in turn, drove prices up to very lofty levels. The market couldn't keep up, and investors who were merely in the market to make some money—many were buying and flipping homes in a very short period of time—began pulling out of the market. Demand started to drop and, so did prices. The collapse of the real estate market in 2007 created an oversupply of houses and decreasing properties prices. Real estate prices depend on the law of supply and demand. When the demand for property is high but property is scarce, prices skyrocket and it becomes a seller's market. When the number of available properties increases to glut the market, prices typically drop. Supply and demand in real estate aren't easy to balance. Creating more saleable properties takes time, considerable work, and a lot of effort. It's not possible at all in some cases, and even when it is, it might not be possible for supply to increase in time to meet consumer demand. So, salespeoples' house sale experiences can also influence the property developer's house sale number.

Understanding this basic economic principle can help consumers decide the best time to buy or sell their properties.

Property market Over-Supply Or Under-Supply factor

You can usually expect a drop in prices when there is an over-supply of homes or land in a given area. You can't move the overage to another area to keep prices stable. Scarcity causes prices to rise when there isn't enough land or if there aren't enough homes in a given area. Even if land is available on which to build more homes, the time it takes to construct them cannot meet immediate property needs, so demand will remain constant or rise. Many forces that might have little or no impact on other regions influence local markets and vice versa. Pay attention to the factors that influence your local market. Watch local businesses and make note of upsizing and downsizing trends if you do business in a market that has jobs and many workers relocating there. You'll also want to keep an eye on these issues if you're a homeowner looking to sell in such an area or if you're looking for property to purchase.

Things like divorce rates, death rates, and demographics can factor in. Factors that can greatly impact property market supply and demand—and by extension your business—might include local weather trends, an aging population, and investment trends if you do business in a resort area that includes vacation homes. Trends that impact discretionary income have more of an influence on this type of market than others. Trends in interest rates, national home prices, new housing starts, and many other economic indicators can influence real estate markets as well. These national events might not typically move real estate supply and demand directly, but they can render it less or more important. The mood and sentiments of the buying public cannot be overlooked. Supply and demand don't exist in a vacuum. But few could afford to pay those prices in a worsening economy and even those who could were understandably reluctant to part with their money at that time. So properties sat on the market, unsold. Worried homeowners in financial distress put their homes up for sale rather than risk foreclosure. Remember, almost 9 million jobs were lost during the Great Recession. Now what happens? Supply begins surpassing demand by leaps and bounds. The housing market is glutted and those healthy prices evaporate—which has little to do with local factors except as they're an extension of national woes.

Land Parcels Are Finite factor to influence property market price

If the country has high population, but land supply is less to let property developers to find lands to build houses easily. Such as Hong Kong is one high population and small city. So, its property prices must be higher to compare other countries, and it causes that its rooms and houses size or area is small , but house sale price or rent is still high.

Such as Hong Kong house market case, Hong Kong people cannot fill a real estate supply shortage by manufacturing more units of land. It's a finite supply, not a manufactured commodity. Hong Kong people might be able to create more units within a given space, such as condos or townhouses, but the land itself is unique and cannot be duplicated to accommodate a short supply. When a shortage of land for homes exists in a given area, Hong Kong people can't simply move in more land to alleviate the shortage. Real estate is where it sits. It will always be a local commodity influenced by local conditions. In short, keep up with the big picture but narrow your primary focus to your region. Supply and demand in real estate will always be foremost a local issue.

As with many other types of business market, the property market is driven by supply and demand. Property prices fluctuate depending upon the factors that influence both supply and demand. Knowledge of these factors equips you with the capability of knowing when to rent/buy and, perhaps just as importantly, when to sell. At the most basic level, when property supply is greater than demand, prices fall. That's the nature of almost every product. Similarly, when the demand for properties is greater than the available supply, prices rise. Even though property markets have these principles in common with many other types of products or business services, there are some differences worth mentioning. For example, the real estate market also takes into consideration factors such as location, seasonality, and durability. There are also different types of real estate – residential, industrial, commercial and land – each of which has their own factors that influence market supply and demand. "Real estate" is defined as more than just property. It also includes natural resources and land, too. So, Hong Kong property market's price is influenced by land supply factor more than other factors, such as facilities , environment , transport etc. factors influence.

Local factors that influence property rates include:

1 – Restrictions on property production – for instance, in the case of Manhatten, there is not much space for added supply. As a result, demand remains high and prices even higher.

2 – Credit access – this often depends on where individuals live. Rural communities may have less access to bank credit, for example – reducing demand.

3 – Job market – the more jobs, the greater the demand for properties.

4 – Transport – better transport translates into greater desirability for people to move – increasing demand.

5 – Retired persons – retired people often decide to downsize and opt for a smaller property in a different locality, thereby increasing supply.

6 – Families – as families begin to grow, they need greater sized properties. This increases the demand for larger homes, whilst decreasing demand for smaller homes.

7 – Meteorology – destinations with more favorable weather profiles and ones that avert the extremes of weather are preferable. Demand in places such as San Diego is significantly higher than the tornado alleys of Alabama.

8 – Income – if income levels in a locality are generally high, there is more money in the market to purchase homes, decreasing supply and increasing prices.

9 – Construction market – the greater the degree of construction of new properties, the greater the supply in the market.

Understanding the factors that drive market supply and demand, and hence property prices are important. The more informed about these nine factors, the better purchasing/selling decisions you can make. For example – designs and styles and fads come and go into "fashion", and what design/style/fad factors elevate a property price one-year can diminish the price of a property the following year. If you are managing a property, you can factor these decisions when determining optimum rent or a selling value.

When borrowing rates are lower, properties become more affordable. This, too, influences demand. Tax credits, for example – for first-time buyers – can encourage more buyers to seek interest in the property market. As well as this, there are various social factors involved, too – such as the social status afforded to people who own their own homes. Age can come into play here, too, depending on the city and what social expectations young professionals have.

What drives property market supply and demand, then, is an interweaving network of factors, many of which playoff on one another. It's important to appreciate the impact that each of these individual factors has and how they influence property prices throughout the country.

How to Analyze Supply and Demand For Apartment Buildings

One of the most important ways to use all of the data gathered in a real estate market analysis is to examine the supply and demand factors for a particular type of real estate. For example, an investor considering the construction or purchase of a new multifamily residential property uses the market analysis to determine what cash flows they can expect to receive given the expected demand for units. The demand must be high enough to generate cash flows that provide a rate of return high enough to make the investment feasible.

In order to estimate the demand for multifamily housing units, it is necessary to understand recent population growth trends for the city. Then, it's important to consider the major industries in the market area and the forecasted growth for those industries over the next few years. You can then put this information together to forecast multifamily housing demand and compare that demand to the existing and proposed supply of multifamily units. This case study takes data about population and industrial activity in the Orlando, Florida region and analyzes supply and demand of multifamily residential units in the region.

Population Trends and Apartment Building Demand

Recent data from the U.S. Census Bureau and the Orlando Economic Development Commission lists the total population of the Orlando metro area at 2,387,138 (2016). Between 2015 and 2016, the population of the Orlando metro area grew by 2.6%. That made Orlando the fastest growing region in the United States. The Orlando Economic Development Commission estimates that population growth in the region since 2000 equates to a gain of 138 people per day. Population growth is mostly fueled by domestic migration. Americans moving to Orlando for retirement in warmer weather or for new career opportunities account for about 40% of the population increase. International migration (mainly from Central and South America) accounts for 34% of the increase in population. People have been moving to the Orlando area due to the region's comparative advantages (climate, entertainment and lifestyle, and economic growth). Without these advantages, Orlando would not be one of the fastest growing regions of the country.

With an average household size around 2.5, that means there are an estimated 954,855 households in the Orlando metropolitan area. Data from the American Consumer Survey indicates that about 43% of the population is renters. So, 43% of households would give an estimated demand of 410,588 multifamily units. In reality, not all renters live in multifamily units since many rent single-family homes. Therefore, it is necessary to estimate how many of those renters occupy multifamily units. A 2016 report from Fannie Mae estimated that there were 156,000 multifamily units in the Orlando metro area with a 5.75% vacancy rate. So, in 2016 there were around 147,030 occupied multifamily units (156,000 x (1-.0575) = 147,030). This means an estimated 35.8% of the households that are renters occupy multifamily units while the remaining 64.2% of renters occupy single-family homes.

Economic Trends and Multifamily Housing Demand

Employment data from the Bureau of Labor Statistics confirms that economic growth is driving the population growth in the Orlando metro area. In fact, job growth from 2015-2016 in Orlando was over twice the national average. A strong economy and growth in the number of jobs indicates that the population should continue to grow over the next few years unless there is a major shift to the national economy or a natural disaster. Furthermore, the job growth rate of 4.22% exceeded the population growth rate of 2.6%. If the major industries in Orlando continue to grow at this pace, more new workers will need to move into the region to fill these new jobs. So, forecasted population growth may be higher than the average of 2% seen over the past 10 years. It might be more appropriate to estimate population growth of at least 3% annually.

As with commodities traded on the market, housing prices continually fluctuate, sometimes with drastic changes over a short period of time. Availability is a huge factor affecting prices within a set region, such as in a specific suburb of a metropolitan area. Likewise, demand for homes in that markct also plays into that pricc, which is why two ncarly idcntical homcs in different cities may sell for vastly different prices. When buying a home in a seller's market, limit your contingencies and make your offer as favorable to the seller as possible.

For houses and virtually anything else available for purchase, supply and demand play into the ultimate selling price. When an item is in short supply and many people want it, prices tend to rise. When the market is flooded with an item or there's no demand for it, prices fall. Sporting event ticket prices tend to rise when a team reaches the championship level, yet tickets to the same team's events a few years later, when the team isn't doing well, cost far less. Prices on holiday decor are another great example: At the peak of any holiday's shopping season, some shoppers are willing to pay a premium for the decor. Three days after the holiday, the leftover stock of these items is marked down to clearance prices due to little demand.

Housing supply and demand works in exactly the same way. Sometimes there are so many single-family homes available in the same region that there aren't enough buyers for all of them. In this housing oversupply, prices drop to draw more attention from potential buyers. A lowered price may influence an interested buyer to choose one home over a similar house in the same general area. Without a lowered price, a house may sit on the market for months due to the abundant number of similar homes for sale nearby at the same time.

On conclusion, property price change can be influenced by house buyers living need and land and house number supply factor, but any house buyer individual rational will influence his/her prerference property choice decision before he / she decides to choose what kinds properties or anywhere locations to live. So, house buyer individual psychological factor will influence his/her properties choices.

How internet influences US and UK property second hand and new house market development ?

What are the factors influence future UK and US property market sale price changes and property supply and demand number changes ? Can internet house advertise influence UK and US second hand and new houses location choice and price variable ? What are the differences between UK and US property market future development trend? Why do UK and US property buyers choose to buy which kinds of property as well as when is the right time to buy UK or US properties by internet channel? I shall explain whether internet is the main factor to influnce UK and US property market price and sale number changes as below:

Some UK property developers estimate these six factors can influence the UK property market future developement.

In UK property market, some property market developers indicate that it could be a better year in Britain's dysfunctional housing market for first-time buyers and tenants. These factors will influence UK property price and sale number increases or decreases to different kinds of properties sale in UK.

1. Interest rates will stay low

Another 0.25% hike is expected in late spring, taking the Bank of England base rate to 0.75%. That will add £22 to the typical £175,000 tracker mortgage, but with more than half of all borrowers on fixed rates, it will probably go unnoticed by most homeowners. With the economy weak, the market does not expect any further hikes across the year. Mortgages will remain cheap although, with inflation outpacing wage rises, will still very much feel like a burden.

2. Housebuilding will rise
New home building has picked up with 217,000 homes coming on to the market in 2016-17, up 20% on the year before. But that only brings the total back to levels seen before the financial crash, and a long way short of the 300,000 target set by the government. If "Brexodus" migration numbers continue to fall and construction activity picks up further, the supply side of the housing equation will be less pressing than in previous years. UK house price growth to slow dramatically in 2018, say experts
3. Landlords will lose out to first-time buyers
First-time buyers should be in the ascendant in 2018, with lending for buy-to-let in retreat. As recently as 2015 landlords snapped up 120,000 houses using buy-to-let finance, but the Council of Mortgage Lenders expects this to fall below 80,000 in 2018. Rising taxes and tougher lending criteria are slowly tipping the balance in favour of homebuyers rather than property speculators.
4. Stamp duty cut and help to buy will continue propping up developers
Stamp duty for all properties up to £300,000 bought by first-time buyers with immediate effect in the budget. The move will save four out of five first-time buyers up to £5,000. But the Office for Budget Responsibility predicts that it will raise prices by 0.3%, with the increase coming in 2018. Meanwhile, the help-to-buy scheme has been given another £10bn boost, providing financing until 2021, although critics say it has been squandered in chasing up the price of new-builds.
5. Tenants may find some relief, at last
After years of galloping rent increases, landlords are finding they can't squeeze tenants any further. Average UK rents rose by less than 1% in 2017, and fell in London. With salaries under pressure from inflation, few expect real rent increases in 2018. Tenants will applaud the new ban on letting agency fees – when it eventually arrives. There is still no date fixed for the ban to come in, but the government insists it will happen some time in 2018.
6. The rich will go higher and higher
The 56 storeys of One Nine Elms will race up London's skyline during 2018, with the first buyers (prices started at £800,000 at launch) moving in in 2019. But its crown as the city's highest residential tower will be swiftly grabbed by the Spire in Docklands. It will have 67 storeys housing 861 suites (many at £2m-plus) and will be completed in 2020.
Hence, future UK properties sale number and price changes, they will depend on above these factors to influence UK property supply number.

So, stamp duty , wage rise level, unemployment level, property geography building choice location, bank lending to property buyers rate , these factors will be main factors to influence UK property supply and demand number and price change in future.

Otherwise, some US property developers estimate these factors can influence the US property market future developement.

- Low mortgage rates will help US homebuyers afford property

Some US property developers believe that bank low mortage rates will excite US property buyers make decision to purchase property desires after 2020. They indicate that whether you're looking to buy or sell a home in 2020 or find the perfect rental, it helps to know what you're up against. In many markets, homebuyers continue to find themselves frustrated, as the relatively few properties coming on the market aren't meeting demand. The likelihood of continued low interest rates make it possible for more individuals to become homeowners for the first time, but fear of a recession and a desire for financial security makes many consumers hesitant to purchase a house.

At the start of 2019, rising interest rates caused many homebuyers to halt their plans for a purchase, as they were unwilling to take on a financial burden they couldn't afford. To ensure buyers remained active, mortgage lenders lowered their interest rates, which have, on average, been below 4% since May for 30-year, fixed-rate mortgages, according to Freddie Mac. They're expected to remain low throughout 2020. Still, some homebuyers are concerned about the future of the economy and their ability to make mortgage payments. Economists largely predict that a recession is still a ways out and not expected until 2021 or later, according to real estate information company Zillow's July 2019 survey of more than 100 real estate and economic experts. However, a segment of the would-be homebuyer market remains skittish.

Although, recession will have indirect relationship to reduce US property buyers' purchase property desires. But concerns about the economy shouldn't inhibit the housing market significantly, or at least not for long. Daryl Fairweather, chief economist for national real estate brokerage Redfin, says the low mortgage rates and the chance to buy a home now as opposed to later will be enough encouragement for homebuyers. "Once they see prices picking up, they're going to get this fear of missing out," she says.But, if Us bank can reduce mortage rate and extend long pay back

mortgage loan time, e.g. from 5 years to 10 years, or 10 years to 20 years. Then US property buyers will feel that they have enough money to buy any new properties, if US banks can reduce mortage loan and extend loan pay back time. Then, bank will excite US property buyers' purchase properties desires in long term. So, home sellers will likely benefit from the number of buyers encouraged by low interest rates, and home prices are expected to continue to trend upward. But don't expect any home price explosions on a large scale.
However, some US propety developers do not believe that bank mortgage low rate factor will excite US property buyers purchase properties desires. They Idon't expect home price appreciation to be much of the story in 2020, but they will see a continuation of what we've been seein. They suggest that home prices should grow and keep sellers and homeowners who are hoping for a rise in their property values happy. But prices should not grow so quickly that markets risk a price correction or buyers hit their price ceiling. There aren't expected to be many sellers in 2020, however. National real estate brokerage Re/Max reports that in October 2019, the inventory for homes for sale was 9% lower than the same month in 2018 across 54 metro areas. The low inventory trend, at least compared to the number of consumers looking to buy, is expected to continue through 2020. Many homeowners locked in low mortgage rates over the past decade, so many don't feel the need to move; they've built equity in their homes and continue to have a low, fixed-rate mortgages with no need to refinance. Plus, the baby boomer population appears to be focused on aging in place rather than downsizing or moving to different accommodations in retirement, Combined with the low mortgage rates they already have on their homes, seniors aren't feeling much incentive to move.

1. US property geographic building location choice factor

The US property geogrpahic building location choice , it will be one factor to influence the area of property sale price and property buyers demand number. For example, the US cities and metro areas where the population is growing fast due to new residents moving in are where you're likely to see home prices increase the most. These markets, which Fairweather notes are more likely to be mid-tier cities in the Midwest or South, such as Charlotte, North Carolina, Charleston, South Carolina, and Richmond, Virginia, that are just a short flight from larger cities like the District of Columbia or Atlanta.The influx of new residents certainly drives up property values as demand increases over the long term, but that means the buyers on the market are more likely to be transplants than lifelong locals. "Any time we see a big increase in migration, prices go up and locals may feel it become unaffordable for them," Fairweather says.

The newest generation in the housing narrative, Generation Z, a group often defined as made up of those born between 1996 and 2010, is largely not ready to purchase a home yet. But expect some 18- to 22 year-olds, the oldest Gen Zers, to be a small portion of the market in 2020. Ryan Gorman, president and CEO of Coldwell Banker NRT, says the Gen Z individuals who are looking to buy now are early adopters, and they're more likely house hunting in small or midsize Midwestern cities where the cost of living is low. "That segment (of the generation) is able to purchase, and the property inventory is there for them to purchase," So, if the geographic location has many young people are living, then the geographic location of property price will may rise, due to there are many young people who have jobs to pay money to buy the geographic location of properties in US some geographic locations , where there are many young people are living in the future US property need market.

Hence, new construction in the outer suburbs of major metro areas appears to promise more affordable options for many first-time homebuyers, though they may have to accept a longer commute for the sake of owning property. It's in these outer suburbs – filled with new construction or existing homes – that many millennial homebuyers are looking to purchase. When these geographic locations have many young people are living and they feel that new construction in the outer suburbs of major metro areas appears to promise more affordable options for many first-time homebuyers, such as young property buyers, they are living in these geographical locations in US.

2. High property material production cost and labor shortage factor can influence property price rises in US property market

Some US property developers believe that property building material cost rises and shortage of labor factor, it can influence property sale price rises, but it can also influence US property buyers purchase properties desires to reduce when they feel US properties prices are sudden risen in the same time. With a large and growing number of homebuyers and a relatively small pool of home sellers, the only saving grace is new construction, which has been notoriously underproducing since the recession. Although new construction appears to be increasing, it still won't be able to meet housing demand. Unfortunately, construction is largely happening in the higher-price tiers, and it's not because (developers) don't want to build on the lower end. Labor shortages and regulatory constraints in many parts of the U.S. mean developers are focusing on properties that will offer the highest yield to offset higher building costs, hence more luxury housing.

3. Long time low renting property to live factor
When US property developers have long time low rent strategy to encourage many US young property buyers, when they feel that they have no enough money to buy houses , buy they can pay long time rent to live in US. Then, the US rent market property renters number will increase. Expect trends in rental rates to remain fairly reactionary to the homebuying market throughout the year, as people examine their financial situation to decide when is the best time to buy. Real estate information and marketing site to US propery rent developers predict that renters who are hesitant or unable to buy a home in their local area will extend their rental agreements, remaining where they are to save as much as possible. Some US property rent developers predict that rents are still expected to grow throughout the year. They predicts that rents will grow faster from the start of the year through the spring, but will slow to 2% year-over-year growth by the end of 2020. They expect to see rental rates rise faster in areas that are seeing significant population growth based on rising demand. However, in parts of the U.S. where home prices will remain affordable, many of these new residents will opt to buy, so rent growth will probably be less significant.

● What Drives US and UK Property Market Supply and Demand
If real estate investing was easy, everyone would be doing it. The truth is, no matter how hard you work on your investment property, there are certain factors driving the real estate market that you simply can't control. These factors will affect everything from housing prices, to the optimal rental strategy, to your potential return on investment. To become a successful real estate investor, you need to be aware of these factors to evaluate how your real estate market is doing and determine whether or not buying an investment property is a smart decision. Here are 4 of these factors:
Factor 1: Demographics
While demographic factors (such as age, race, gender, and median income) are often overlooked, they're actually significant to property investors. Such factors will help you anticipate real estate market trends which, in turn, will

influence your investment decision. For example, knowing that a certain area is home to aging baby boomers and retirees or is attractive to young millennials starting families and building their careers will give you a better understanding of your prospective buyers/renters. This will also affect the best type of rental property to invest in and what to look for in an investment property.

Demographic factors also have a tendency to affect the housing market in terms of demand. Property investors should be aware of whether the population is increasing or shrinking. Simply ask yourself: Are people moving into or out of the city? If you're a real estate investor depending on rental income, this is a crucial factor to take into account. Investing in an area with a growing population means a larger pool of potential tenants and higher occupancy rates. Moreover, when the demand in a real estate market increases, so will home prices and rental rates. As a result, you can charge tenants of your rental properties higher rents and make a good return on investment.

Factor 2: Economic Conditions

There's a positively correlated relationship between the economy and the real estate market – when one rises, the other rises as well, and when one falls, so does the other. This is why the economy gets blamed for every real estate downturn. First of all, the overall health of the economy plays a major role in the value of real estate properties. Secondly, the job market contributes the amount of money available for people to buy homes. A city with a stable and growing job market will have a stable and growing housing market.Job market growth, by itself, is an important factor seeing as it's tied to the increase in population – markets offering more job opportunities will attract new residents. Moreover, if you're investing in a rental property in a growing housing market, charging higher rents becomes more reasonable because tenants won't have trouble paying. Therefore, property investors should look at the employment rate and projected job growth in the real estate market and, using our property finder tool, find the best rental properties for sale in the city.

Factor 3: Supply of Homes

For many reasons, property investors should keep a close eye on supply vs. demand. To begin with, this determines whether a real estate market is a seller's or buyer's market. Additionally, a shortage of supply will push up rental property prices while, on the other hand, a surplus of supply will cause prices to fall. Simple economics. Knowing this will influence your investment decisions whether as a seller or a buyer.

Is the 2018 US Housing Market a Seller's Market or a Buyer's Market? A smart real estate investor will also watch out for future construction and buildings coming to the housing market. You want to ensure that the supply of housing will be able to keep up with the increasing demand as more and more people move to the city. At the same time, you don't want to invest where there are more units built than people coming into the housing market because this could mean high vacancy rates. Experts believe that a healthy real estate market has 4 – 6 months of inventory.

Factor 4: Geographic Location

The geographic location where the investment property sits also has its influences on the housing market – it explains why some cities are more expensive than others. For example, Los Angeles, Seattle, and San Francisco face hard physical boundaries like coastlines and mountains, which limits the real estate market's capacity for expansion, making it more expensive. You'd also notice that a waterfront home is usually priced higher than one not on the water. This is because investing in such rental properties is riskier due to the geography, and a real estate investor would have to put more on property insurance. Many also believe that climate change has affected property prices in cities like New York and Miami.

Climate Change and Rising Real Estate Prices: Is There a Connection? With location comes school districts, which also affect home prices. The school district (or even a specific school within a district) can drive demand in the housing market. Any real estate agent will confirm that investing in a district that has strong schools can affect home prices by as much as 10%. As with many other types of business market, the property market is driven by supply and demand. Property prices fluctuate depending upon the factors that influence both supply and demand.

Knowledge of these factors equips you with the capability of knowing when to rent/buy and, perhaps just as importantly, when to sell. At the most basic level, when property supply is greater than demand, prices fall. That's the nature of almost every product. Similarly, when the demand for properties is greater than the available supply, prices rise. Even though property markets have these principles in common with many other types of products or business services, there are some differences worth mentioning. For example, the real estate market also takes into consideration factors such as location, seasonality, and durability. There are also different types of real estate – residential, industrial, commercial and land – each of which has their own factors that influence market supply and demand. “Real estate” is defined as more than just property. It also includes natural resources and land, too.

● Property supply and demand is driven by both local and general factors.

There are nine local factors that Influence Supply/Demand to US and UK property market as below: Local factors that influence property rates include:

1 – Restrictions on property production – for instance, in the case of Manhatten, there is not much space for added supply. As a result, demand remains high and prices even higher.

2 – Credit access – this often depends on where individuals live. Rural communities may have less access to bank credit, for example – reducing demand.

3 – Job market – the more jobs, the greater the demand for properties.

4 – Transport – better transport translates into greater desirability for people to move – increasing demand.

5 – Retired persons – retired people often decide to downsize and opt for a smaller property in a different locality, thereby increasing supply.

6 – Families – as families begin to grow, they need greater sized properties. This increases the demand for larger homes, whilst decreasing demand for smaller homes.

7 – Meteorology – destinations with more favorable weather profiles and ones that avert the extremes of weather are preferable. Demand in places such as San Diego is significantly higher than the tornado alleys of Alabama.

8 – Income – if income levels in a locality are generally high, there is more money in the market to purchase homes, decreasing supply and increasing prices.

9 – Construction market – the greater the degree of construction of new properties, the greater the supply in the market.

● Prediction property market trend within one to two year in demand and supply theory analysis

Understanding the factors that drive market supply and demand, and hence property prices are important.The more informed about these factors, the better purchasing/selling decisions you can make. Of course, there are more than just local factors to consider. There are some general factors to think about, too. What’s ahead for our property markets in the next year or two? Some property developers apply demand and supply theory to analyze the US and UK property price how is influenced to change by the supply and demand to UK and US property market within next one to two year .

(1) Property design or fashion factor

For example – designs and styles and fads come and go into "fashion", and what design/style/fad factors elevate a property price one-year can diminish the price of a property the following year. If you are managing a property, you can factor these decisions when determining optimum rent or a selling value.

(2) Borrowing rare factor

When borrowing rates are lower, properties become more affordable. This, too, influences demand. Tax credits, for example – for first-time buyers – can encourage more buyers to seek interest in the property market. As well as this, there are various social factors involved, too – such as the social status afforded to people who own their own homes. Age can come into play here, too, depending on the city and what social expectations young professionals have.

What drives property market supply and demand, then, is an interweaving network of factors, many of which playoff on one another. It's important to appreciate the impact that each of these individual factors has and how they influence property prices throughout the country. House prices across all our capital cities are expected to grow over 2020/21. The combination of lower interest rates, easing lending serviceability buffers and increased consumer sentiment is expected to bring more buyers back into the market. And with property values rising, sellers (who have generally been on strike) will slowly return to the market increasing stock levels. We know the Reserve Bank is hell bent on decreasing unemployment and pushing up wages and that means it's likely interest rates will fall further in 2020. However the pace of property price recovery may be limited because, while interest rate serviceability thresholds for most borrowers has been reduced, lenders are expected to maintain their more conservative approach towards assessing borrower income and expenses. However, various commentators have offered different forecasts for what's ahead in 2020.

● What are the main factors influence the future England and America property market future development

Firstly, I shall discuss whether what what are the main factors to influence UK future property development market. the main factors influence UK future property market development, they many include demographic (living culture) and baby boomer (population growth) both aspects as belo:

1. Demographic Trends and how they affect Property Investment Potential factor. Demographics means 'the quantity and characteristics of the people who live in a particular area, especially in relation to their age, how much money they have and what they spend it on.

European Demographics

The UK has one of the better demographic trends for house prices compared to other countries, with average families of 1.8 and a net immigration. However, both Spain and Italy have only 1.2 and the population of Italy is forecast to reduce to 40 million in the next 30 years from 55 million in the 1990s. This will certainly not help demand and for this reason we would be very cautious about buying property in Italy . Spain has 1.2 though the net flux of foreigners buying holiday homes is huge hence property in the south coastal area where population is increasing should stay firm, though we wonder whether Madrid will go into the doldrums?

Otherwise, in Germany , the situation is not good – the eastern German people in particular have not been having large families and the German population will decline. Both the Netherlands and Scandinavia are more healthy. The theory is that for women in the more traditional, often Catholic, cultures in the south of Europe, child minding is either not available or very expense and difficult to find – couples have tried to both work and this has lead to families starting later, being smaller and sometimes not starting at all. It's a complex social phenomenon with many facets, but if you go north and west in Europe , it seems people have larger families – may be it's all those cold dark rainy nights in winter! There is also the reluctance or not of government to allow immigration – the UK has always been a country with reasonably high immigration levels which has helped support and increase population levels – this is not the case in countries like Italy and Austria . For this reason, we see increasing population in the north western areas of Europe, decreases in much of south and eastern Europe and selective increases in holiday destinations where some foreign retired people or holiday homers will settle (e.g. southern Spain, southern France, Greece, Cyprus, a few spots in Italy e.g. Sorrento).These demographics have to be considered when property investing, since of course they tend to drive the demand side of the supply/ demand equation, albeit in theory one can still have a declining population and increased demand if everyone decides to have more than one home.

European Demographic Changes up to 2050

Property investment is for most people a long-term financial undertaking – so with this in mind, it seems prudent to consider future long-term demographic changes that will affect supply and demand for property in Europe up until 2050. A hundred years ago, the European population was 14% of the world's population. Today this is down to 6%. By 2050 it is forecast by the United Nations to be 4%. The UN predict the population of the EU will contract by 7.5 million people over the next 45 years – this assumes that there will also be a net immigration of 6.8 million – hence the indigenous population will decline by some 14 million. In the USA the population will grow by 40% in the same period.

It is not increasing mortality but the low fertility rates in many European countries that will be responsible for this shrinkage. People are getting married later, having fewer kids and many only have one or even no children. If the Italians keep their low fertility rate, and there is not a significant rise in immigration, the UN forecasts the population will drop by 30%. In Eastern European countries, the population is forecast to drop by 25% in the next 45 years. That said, the prices are likely to rise significantly in most of these countries the next few years as most of them join the EU, but in the longer term we would be very careful since demand will most likely be reduced for all but the nicest retirement property as the population dwindles. Otherwise, the median age of the Greeks, Italians and Spaniards is projected to exceed 50 by 2050 – one in three people will be over 65 years old. Clearly to pay for these retired people, either taxes will have to go up to say 75%, or state pensions and health care expenditure will have to be drastically reduced. In NW Europe, the situation is more healthy - in the UK , Scandinavia, Holland , Belgium and to a lesser extent France . But in eastern and southern European countries, there will be a significant decline in the population.

2. Baby boomer: 'somebody born during a baby boom, especially the one following the end of World War II'. The UK population is projected to increase from some 55 million in 1975 to 68+ million by 2020, mainly through people living longer. Much of this population growth is in the south-east of England . Even though we are not reproducing ourselves (average family couples have 1.8 offspring in 2003 instead of the 2.2 need to keep the population replicating), people are living far longer than

previously mainly due to improved health care, working conditions and less pollution – albeit counter to this trend is that fact that most people get less exercise and are more overweight than 50 years ago. If this trend is reversed, one could expect to see average ages and hence the population grow even higher.

Another important trend is immigration – these families tend to have more children when they settle and hence support population growth – something which is healthy for supporting higher GDP growth and preventing wage inflationary pressures building (which can in turn lead to higher interest rates). This general demographic situation is well known, fairly deterministic and should help support house prices and demand for property in the longer term. On a small scale, expect the following demographic trends on a UK regional level.

As baby boomers retire, they will move out of city suburbs to be close to the sea or in leisure areas such as national parks, though most will try and stay close to their families and friends. Continued strong economic activity in the major service centres will lead to increasing populations and wealth e.g. London , Manchester , Leeds . Many rural areas that are not considered good retirement centres may continue to depopulate as farming becomes more difficult (e.g. northern Scotland, mid Wales) – though the people that move in may be wealthy ex-city workers wanting a lifestyle change. Many retiring baby-boomers will relocate to southern coastal areas in England and Wales where the weather is slightly warmer and scenery un-spoilt.

City centre living and pied-de-terres will become more popular as amenities (e.g. healthcare) and cultural activities improve for both young and elderly people – many commuters will become tired of long daily commutes and have two properties – one in the country, one in the city. Lifestyle shifting – wealthy middle classes moving from London to Cornwall , Devon, Dorset select country areas. So there will be a shift of low earning rural people to the cities/suburbs and wealthy city folk to the countryside – buying farms and leasing out the land to merged mega-farms. There will be a considerable increase in demand for homes (whether permanent or second homes) with sea/coastal views as the baby boomers retire starting in 2004 (the oldest baby boomer is now 58 years old) and continuing for the next 20 years.

● Why does UK property market demand grow up by baby boomer to 2050 ?

Based on these projections of an aging population, we have prepared a few types of property that will be in demand, and those that will not be in

demand as this demographic shift takes place from now until 2050:
Some UK property developers indicate that the baby boomer factor may influence property In UK property demand increases may include these elements on property design demand or living need aspect:

UK property living increase demand

Secure luxury apartments in nice neighbourhoods close to city centres in UK (mainly in the south – e.g. London , Southampton, Portsmouth , Bristol , Bath), Scandinavia and France. Medium sized bungalows and holiday homes on the south coast of NW European countries – UK , Norway , Sweden , France – suitable for retirement. Luxury apartments, villas and holiday homes in tourist areas on the southern coast of Spain, Greek islands, Italy – western coast, south of France, Balkan coastal area, Cyprus, east coast of Bulgaria. Rural retreats in France – bought by wealthy retiring UK and Dutch citizens. Quality medium sized home in the England and south Wales in secure areas in market towns, historic university towns and villages – the further south the more popular

Seaside property with sea views along south coast of England – e.g. Cornwall , Devon , Sussex .

UK Property Not in demand

Large suburban houses in average areas in cities in Spain , Austria , Switzerland , Italy , Portugal , Greece , eastern European countries and Germany. Village and rural homes in eastern European countries that are not close to airports and amenities and cannot be classified as either holiday, second or retirement homes. "Run of the mill" family homes with many bedrooms in areas not close to good amenities, health care, city centre culture and tourist attractions. Property in expensive country areas in Italy and Germany and city suburban property particularly inland in the colder and more industrial north of the countries (e.g. Milan, Turin, Hamburg, Essen, Saxony) will likely see stagnating house prices since economic growth will be anaemic as the baby boomers retire, populations decrease, wage earnings growth is low and taxes increase to pay for the retired.

In European countries where wages and the standard of living is still rising, one can expect to see prices moving up towards the Italian level – examples of such countries are Spain, Greece, Slovenia. However, after they have caught up, unless the property is a good home suitable for a local or international retiring baby-boomer, we would not advise investing in this.

"Baby Boomers" Demographics and Desires to UK future property development growth

A key consideration in future property investments is how will the baby boomers affect market prices and demand, and which segments will this be in? The baby boomers are those born between mid 1946 (end the World War II) and 1964. This was an unprecedented baby boom period in the UK , Europe and the USA . Immediately after the war, a surge in babies resulted from servicemen arriving home late 1945 and this continued at rather high levels until the early 1960s (peaking in the late 1950s). It led to the house building boom of the late 1950s and 1960s when 3-4 bedroomed houses were built in suburban areas to house rapidly expanding families.

These baby boomers are just starting to retire now – the first wave are now 58 years old in 2004 – most retire between 60 and 65 years old. In the next twenty years there will be a huge opportunity to service these baby boomers – they are the ones who have benefited most from the boom economic years and have already driven house prices to record highs. They are currently in their peak money generating years (40s and early 50s). So what next? My prediction is that these baby boomers will want the following:

These new baby boomers will “not” want to sit out their retirement – most will be active, sporty, fit, desire the café culture, want to travel extensively, and be independent. They will “not” desire boring warden assisted retirement complexes in the middle of nowhere – what they “will” desire is fun, the sea, a community and proximity to family, friends and culture. They will avoid high crime areas, want to be close to airports and avoid traffic jams. They may also desire to return to where they or their family grew-up if they had fond memories, or move to where they enjoyed family holidays. In summary, they are likely to either:

Have a second home in a holiday resort – probably at the coast (sun, sea, sand, sailing)

Have a secure apartment in a town or city centre with culture (e.g. Paris , London , Barcelona)

Many UK property developers believe the ideal investment to service these needs is a medium-high end two double bedroomed apartment with balcony overlooking the sea or marina (example locations would be the south coast of England or Spain etc). There will be more and more baby boomers chasing less and less property – and it’s just beginning. The suburban semi-detached and detached houses – so called commuter properties – will probably become less fashionable. Large houses in the countryside with land will probably increase their value, although these properties may become difficult for the elderly people to maintain and service in later years. They also believe the biggest increase could be in coastal areas where property prices have not risen too much already and are being gentrified. Some of these are the old Victorian seaside resorts. Now Brighton has already tripled in price, because of its proximity to London , culture, historic houses and seaside / marina. But there are many other such old resorts that are less than half the price. These include Hastings , Folkestone, Margate/ Broadstairs, Bexhill and Eastbourne . Any improvement in infra-structure in these towns will improve things further – examples are the new arts University in Hastings , new high speed train link from Folkestone to London St Pancras. Other places to benefit should be Chatham/Rochester, Whitstable and Gravesend . As more baby boomers settle in these coastal towns, the café culture should improve, crime levels reduce and gentrification kick-in.

Many UK property deverlopers see particular capital growth in these areas in the next 10-15 years, as more baby boomers decide to settle outside urban conurbations to the "seaside". The sea, sand, sun, surfing, sailing, walking, cycling, café culture and activities / amenities will increase demand in these areas. That is not to say that the main city centres will not do well. Baby boomers may also choose to have a pied-de-terre for tourism, leisure, maintaining business and investment contacts, visiting family and friends – hot areas are likely to be Bow, Hackney, Bethnal Green, Stratford , Canning Town and Silvertown in London along with established prime areas in West London such as Kensingon, Chelsea , Bayswater and Battersea/ Clapham and Fulham. These properties are likely to be secure semi-luxury apartments in good central locations

- Factors That Affect House Prices In UK

If we study the house price chart of UK we would come to know that there had been a rise in prices during the early 00's. Then a huge decline is seen during 2004-05.A small recovery was seen after that but the major downfall in house prices struck in 20 08. 2008-09 brought changes in house prices and it was quiet obvious since the world faced one of the worst slump in the history. Due to this recession almost every sector was affected. Since everything in our society is linked to each other the houses prices were affected too.

UK House prices are affected by a combination of supply and demand factors.

Demand Side Factors:

1. Economic Growth / Real income.

Improved life standards enable people to earn more and spend more. Few years back people use to have a mortgage ratio of 3 times your salary. For example if a person earns £30,000 the building society would lead £90,000. Therefore rising incomes enable house prices to rise. However, the ratio of house prices to income can vary considerably. For example, between 1995 and 2007, the ratio of house prices to incomes have increased significantly. If the economy goes into a recession and unemployment rises, the demand for buying houses would fall significantly.

2. Consumer confidence

During times of high consumer confidence, people are more willing to take out risky mortgages to be able to buy a house. In the period 2001-07 100% mortgages and interest only mortgages were quite common. In the early 00s, people were optimistic about the housing market and so took out mortgages with a higher debt to income ratio. The economic boom during the early 00s gave the people enough confidence to take loan with even higher interest rates. Since the unemployment was quiet low the consumers had confidence about their earnings. This confidence is clearly reflected in the increase in real estate business during early 00s.

3. Interest rates.

From past few years Interest rate was low. To counter off the inflationary effect bank of England had to increase the interest rates, thus increase the interest rates in the financial markets. The economic recession created a severe credit crunch thus providing the basis for huge crash in real estate markets. For example, America is the country which was severely hit by the credit crunch crises. In simple words people were issued loans on the basis of just there pay slips. Though the lands and mortgaged property was taken as security but this was not enough for what future explained. Rise in oil prices proved to be one of the main causes of economic recession ultimately giving rise to unemployment. Thus people went jobless and were unable to pay the mortgage installments. Real estate markets had crashed due to lack in demand and excess supply, since the banks wanted to auction the property for recovery of mortgaged amount.

Interest rates affect the cost of paying for a mortgage. Interest rates are very important as mortgage repayments are usually the biggest part of a homeowner's monthly spending. In the UK, the majority of homeowners have a variable mortgage which means increase in interest rate would surely effect the buying's. The rise in interest rates proved to be significant event in drop in houses demand. People on fixed rate mortgages will be insulated from fluctuating rates for 2-10 years. Therefore changes in interest rates can have a time lag of upto 18months before there full effect is noted on demand for housing. It is also important to consider real interest rates (interest rates-inflation). The Bank of England set base rates and these usually affect all commercial rates. However, sometimes the Bank of England cut interest rates, but, commercial banks don't pass these cuts onto consumers. In the first half of 2008, the Bank of England cut rates by 0.5% from 5.5 to 5.0%, but the cost of mortgages is still rising.

4. Availability of Mortgage Finance

From 1970s to 80s of twentieth century the loan culture was not much common, later by increase in financial institutions & with deregulation of the banking sector increased competition has seen a rise in the number of mortgage products. Products such as interest only, self certification mortgages and mortgages up to 6 times income have enabled people to get more mortgages, thereby increasing demand for housing. However, during the credit crunch of 2008, the number of mortgage products on offer fell due to a shortage of finance in the money markets. This credit crunch has surely proved severe downfall in house prices. Neither people have enough money to buy houses nor are loans available. Loans are provided on higher interest rates.

5. Demographic factors

There have been a rising number of households in the UK. The number of households can rise faster than the population if the average family size decline and there are more single people living alone. If we study UKs population chart the earning ages have declined to 16 or 17 which means more people are earning and getting independent. This independence gives rise to house buyers.

Demand for housing in the UK has been increasing for various reasons such as:

An increase in divorce rates

Ultimately rising the demands for separate house. The immigration from east Europe And the eastern countries give rise in the demand of houses in UK. Increase in life expectancy and more old single people. Children leaving home early for earning and a thought of getting independent.

Speculation

There are many people in UK who buy houses for the capital gains. The uncertainty in market and rise in unemployment has drawn all eyes away from this business. Increase in interest rates has even attracted the investors to save their money to earn interest. Not everyone buys a house to live in it. An increasing number of property investors buy houses to try and make both capital gains and income from renting. This buy to let investor is typically more volatile, they will buy when house prices are rising and sell when the market appears to turn. This makes house prices more volatile because speculators will buy in a boom and sell in a bust. The number of buy to let investors in the UK has risen in the past decade.

However, there are quite high fixed costs in selling a house, such as stamp duty and estate agent fees. It is not like dealing in shares where you can easily buy and sell. Many buy to let investors claim they are in for the long term.

The price of rented accommodation

Although UK house prices have increased faster than inflation, renting has also become expensive which is the main substitute to buying a house.

Inherited wealth

Increase in life expectancies has decreased the death rates and hence the inherited wealth is distributed lately blocking the amount for a longer time.Division of properties divide the money too. Thus more people get the money to invest. Low unemployment is often associated with rising demand for houses.

Supply side Factors

In the short run Supply of housing is fixed because it takes time to build houses. Therefore in the short run demand affects prices more than supply. However if the supply of housing is inelastic then an increase in demand will lead to a big increase in price. The above given factors give us an idea that due to slow pace of house building prices are consistent and do not show any kind of variation. The current situation do not satisfy these conditions because currently inflation has caused the material prices to increase rapidly, rising the house prices.

In the long Run the supply of UK housing is affected by many factors as below:

At times investments are blocked in the rural areas due to restriction by government. Building houses and buildings is a time taking process. Investors hesitate to invest because a huge amount is blocked in construction. UK has many homes which were built many years ago. Now these houses are being demolished and flats are given priority over the houses giving rise in supply of houses.An increase in the cost of building new houses will shift supply to the left.

In the UK, it is argued there is a significant shortage of housing is this explains why house prices have risen much faster than inflation and earnings. However, in the US, the supply of housing increased in the period upto 2008 and therefore, the excess supply and falling demand led to a big fall in demand. However, it is important to note that house prices can still fall, even if there is a shortage of supply. In 1992, house prices in London fell over 20%, even though we can say supply is inelastic. A shortage of supply just means they will be on average higher. It doesn't mean they are incapable of falling.

US property market development will influence by these below factors

Secondly, I shall discuss whether what what are the main factors to influence US future property development market needs.

In its annual look ahead, the Urban Land Institute predicts a soft landing. That may seem totally tone-deaf when considering today's news cycle and the overall tumult of 2017 thus far. But as far as the real estate industry is concerned, the immediate future promises a relatively smooth ride. Unveiled during the organization's annual fall meeting in Los Angeles this morning, the 2018 Emerging Trends in Real Estate report, a joint project between ULI and PricewaterhouseCoopers researchers, compiles more than 800 individual interviews and 1,600 surveys from a diverse array of real estate, economic, and development professionals. It's been anything but a slow year, with an expanding affordable-housing shortage, cries of a new urban crisis impacting cities, a string of tragic and costly natural disasters, and new regulatory and tax uncertainty due to proposed Trump administration policy. But the consensus of real estate experts and analysts surveyed by ULI views a "sudden drop in altitude" as highly unlikely. Growth trends and an economic tailwind suggest an expansion of the current cycle, amid larger structural shifts in real estate.

The housing shortage offers opportunities

Forget new billion-dollar tech startups: The real unicorns in today's economy may be mid-priced single-family homes that a cross-section of buyers can actually afford. No segment of the housing market has so many potential buyers, just no scalable solution remains so elusive, due to a number of economic factors. Experts zeroed in on this difficult, yet in-demand housing as perhaps the most valuable, and vexing, product to develop. Whether it's urban row houses, transit-oriented development, or a new type of tract housing, practical and affordable mid-market homes, as well as starter homes and affordable rental units for young adults, remain potential goldmines for developers who figure out the right balance of price, land costs, location, and amenities. The higher-end market remains well-served. While margins are still good for those types of projects, building affordable housing at scale, in nearly any urban market in the country, would be welcome.

Are fears of another recession or crash misplaced? The regular economic cycle suggests the U.S. economy is due for a correction, yet, according to experts cited in the trends report, the immediate future may resemble a smooth-glide path as opposed to a nose dive. Most investors have lived through a few hard landings in the recent past—the savings-and-loan collapse of the '80s, the dot-com bubble, and the Great Recession—but this time, many see something different. Many in the industry point to signs, such as the very low unemployment rate, a policy shift toward tightening at the Fed, and high asset prices in real estate, as positive indications that investors are getting more defensive and conservative as the cycle stretches out. By achieving more balance, the market may have reached a "new normal" of slow and steady growth.

Productivity of commercial property number supply factor

Both as a social imperative and a business necessity in an ever-tightening labor market—has put more and more pressure on office workers, and offices, to perform. Developers and commercial-property owners need to focus on providing not just space and a great location, but an environment for success.

Office or house design factor

As office design morphs into more mixed workspaces, and the tech world fetish for innovation, creative commons, and innovation bleeds into every sector of the economy, more and more firms want curated, configured office spaces that boost productivity. Developers who focus on and market design and efficiency, and tailor their products to ever-evolving workplace trends (flexibility, green design, smart office space), will benefit greatly. Tired of trend stories about how millennials are reshaping the housing market? Thankfully, a new demographic has emerged on the radar of economists and trend forecasters, ready for its own moment under the microscope. Gen Z, defined variously as the generation born starting anywhere from 1995 to 2001, is predicted to hit the post-college housing market in much the same way as millennials, loaded with debt and preferring a more urban lifestyle.

They'll also enter the working world looking for structure and stability; researchers suggests they're both more competitive and more easily distracted. But before they make their full impact felt in the office or housing markets, they'll likely have a much greater effect on retail and shopping. Their "gadgeteria" ethos and social-media second nature will put more and more pressure on retailers and retail landlords to create experiential stores with connectivity that respond to individual preferences.

Baby boomers population growth factor

Initial predictions that the baby boomers would already be retiring en masse at fancy retirement communities and active lifestyle developments have given way to a more complicated reality, shaped in large part by fallout from the Great Recession. Additional loan burdens and a lack of financial planning and savings have put many boomers in an awkward position, causing some to delay retirement. A 2016 survey showed that 37 percent of boomers had less than $50,000 in savings.

While the high end of the market will seek out urban living, an active lifestyle, and luxury rentals, many others will scramble to locate affordable housing options fit for aging in place. Real estate professionals will need to overcome a number of challenges to capitalize on this huge market, one that survey participants said was one of the most promising residential sectors in 2018, including helping many boomers sell their large homes (which may not have the amenities millennials want), and then helping them downsize or find affordable housing options for their golden years.

By 2030, 75.5 million Americans will be over the age of 65, with a vast diversity of needs, financial situations, and lifestyle preferences. Other than its vast size, this is a market that defies easy categorization. US Urban Land Institute indicated that the U.S. property these different geographical property overall and investment investment rank in 2018 as below:

U.S. Markets to Watch in 2018

Market Overall Rank Investment Rank Development Rank

Seattle 1 2 1

Austin 2 3 2

Salt Lake City 3 1 10

Raleigh/Durham 4 4 4

Dallas/Fort Worth 5 6 5

Fort Lauderdale 6 16 3

Los Angeles 7 8 8

San Jose 8 11 9

Nashville 9 5 13
Boston 10 9 14
Miami 11 18 6
Charlotte 12 12 16
Portland 13 7 20
Charleston 14 17 12
Washington, D.C. 15 10 21
Orlando 16 21 11
Atlanta 17 15 15
San Antonio 18 13 18
Tampa/St.
Petersburg 19 27 7
Oakland/East
Bay 20 20 19
It's different this time: Secondary markets refuse to be afterthoughts.
Secondary property market development future
In the U.S. have outpaced the primary cities, at least according to survey results from the Urban Land Institute, leading analysts to suggest there's a lot more staying power here than years past. The reasons are varied: Investors are better educated, secondary markets haven't become as overbuilt as they were in previous cycles, foreign capital has grown and seeks a safe home, and the growth in many of these cities seems much more sustainable and long-lasting. After lagging behind in the recovery, secondary markets seem poised for growth and continued appreciation, making it a good time to invest.
When it came to predicting where investment and growth are headed, analysts favored so-called second cities. The report's predictions for the hottest markets of 2018 favored many secondary markets, with Seattle surging on Amazon-backed growth to a top ranking. Miami also made a huge jump from 25 to 11 in the rankings. Primary markets took a beating, with only LA and Boston in the top 10, and both San Francisco (27) and Manhattan (46) taking steep drops.

US property technological design factor
Is housing at a technological tipping point?. The oft-dismissed sci-fi nature of high-tech construction, such as prefab homes and 3D printing, has progressed beyond mere hype and hope. With demand rising and ever-present labor shortages showing no signs improving soon, new technologies, and the efficiency, progressive workflows, construction

automation, and processes they can bring, will be embraced by the industry. While many worksites are just beginning to benefit from improved worksite tech, better workflows, and safer job sites, extensive activity on the fringes of the homebuilding industry suggests a more impactful breakthrough is imminent.

US tax reform factor

While tax reform, at the present moment, still has a lengthy road to legislative success, the proposed overhaul has numerous potential impacts on the real estate world. Many suggested cuts and changes bear close watch by the real estate industry. Low-income housing tax credits (LIHTCs) may be on the docket, an extremely troubling development for affordable housing. Other proposals to double the standard deduction on personal income, alter investment amortization, and get rid of the 1031 tax-free exchange program would add disruptions and numerous potential ripple effects.

- The main influential Housing Market Factors influence US future property market development in supply and demand view

The housing market is a key component to the entire U.S. economy. Having said that, nearly everyone should have an interest in the direction of the housing sector. It is a rather prominent indicator as to the direction the country is heading. However, for those invested in the industry, it hits home on a more personal level. Homeowners, and investors in particular, are at the mercy of the housing market – good or bad as it may be. If you already own a home, you are well aware of the impact a particular market cycle has on net worth. If you are in the process of buying a home, the market will dictate how much you will have to pay. To help you understand what drives home prices, this article will address four factors that have an impact on the housing market.

Supply and Demand to US property development market

As perhaps the most basic concept of economics, supply and demand will dictate the direction of the housing market.The more houses that are available at a given time, the less competition there will be. Conversely, if a desirable neighborhood is void of sellers, the prices will rise, as more people will be competing over the same properties. Supply and demand will result in one of two market conditions:

A Sellers Market: When the market demand for properties in a particular area is high and when there is a shortage of good quality properties (i.e. supply is scarce) then the balance of power in the market shifts towards the seller. This is because there is likely to be excess demand in the market for good properties. Sellers can wait for offers on their property to reach (or exceed) their minimum selling price.

A Buyers Market: Conversely when demand both for new and older housing is weak and when there is a glut of properties available on the market, then the power switches to potential buyers. They have a much wider choice of housing available and they should be able to negotiate a price that is lower than the published price.

Of course, the housing market is not always so easy to delineate between the two. It can be very difficult to determine all of the factors that impact supply and demand. For example, it is possible for prices to rise in a neighborhood where there is a large amount of available inventory if the demand is high enough. Therefore, it is important to understand what factors are affecting demand, right down to the smallest detail. This could include a local school district, or even a transit system.

Interest Rates influence US property buyers property purchase desire

With the cost of homes in today's market, it is not uncommon to require the assistance of a lender. While the best investors prefer paying cash, the average investor will need the cooperation of a lending institution. Having said that, interest rates play a major role in the purchasing of a home, and subsequently the entire housing market. Low interest rates, in particular, can positively affect the demand for housing. Paying less on your mortgage is an attractive incentive. Those who are on the fence may be swayed into purchasing a home if interest rates are low enough. As for those that already own a home, they may be encouraged to upgrade if rates are conducive to the trade up. When rates are rapidly increasing, there may be a surge in sales as buyers attempt to close deals before they are squeezed out of the market due to higher borrowing costs. While this is true, if rates continue to rise, they will likely reach a point where they become a burden. Of the factors that impact the housing sector, mortgage rates are the one aspect that buyers have some influence over as an individual. There are steps you can take to make sure you get the best mortgage rate. In fact, buyers with great credit (mid-700s and above) will qualify for the best rates.

Availability of Funds influences US property purchase buyers desire

As discussed, low interest rates can prompt significant activity within the housing sector. However, those rates are of little help if a borrower is unable to secure funding in the first place. Financial institutions are not interested in making loans without considering the risk involved. If there is a weak or declining economy, buyers with marginal credit or relatively low personal cash flow may find it especially difficult to obtain a loan. When the economy is booming, lending standards may be loosened and the housing market can be further stimulated.

The Stock Market impacts US property purchase buyers deisre

The stock market has a major impact on the entire economy as a whole. Therefore, it should come as no surprise to learn that the performance of the stock market dictates the direction of the housing sector. The same holds true for those that don't even have any investments directly tied into the market itself. Since most people participate in the stock market in some way, it is a factor that impacts the vast majority of potential and current homeowners. This doesn't even account for the psychological impact a poorly performing market can have on the greater population.

References and Further Reading

Camerer, C., Loewenstein, G., & Prelec, D. (2005) Neuroeconomics: How neuroscience can inform economics. Journal of Economic Literature, 43, 9-64.

Coulter, K. S., & Coulter, R. A. (2005). Size does matter: The effects of magnitude representation congruency on price perceptions and purchase likelihood. Journal of Consumer Psychology, 15(1), 64–76.

Diamond, A. (2013). Executive functions. Annual Review of Psychology, 64, 135-168.

Diclemente, C. C., Marinilli, A. S., Singh, M., & Bellino, L. E., (2001). The role of feedback in the process of health behavior change. American Journal of Health Behavior, 25, 217-227.

Dolan, P., Hallsworth, M., Halpern, D., King, D., & Vlaev, I. (2010). MINDSPACE: Influencing behaviour through public policy. London, UK: Cabinet Office.

Finucane, M. L., Alhakami, A., Slovic, P., & Johnson, S. M. (2000). The affect heuristic in judgments of risks and benefits. Journal of Behavioral Decision Making, 13, 1-17.

Golman, R., Hagmann, D., & Loewenstein, G. (2017). Information avoidance. Journal of Economic Literature, 55(1), 96-135.

Iyengar, S., & Lepper, M. (2000). When choice is demotivating: Can one desire too much of a good thing? Journal of Personality and Social Psychology, 79, 995-1006.

Kahneman, D. (2011). Thinking, fast and slow. London: Allen Lane.

Loewenstein, G. (2000). Emotions in economic theory and economic behavior. The American Economic Review, 90(2), 426-432.

Rick, S. I. (2018). Tightwads and spendthrifts: An interdisciplinary review. Financial Planning Review, 1(1-2), e1010. Retrieved from https://doi.org/10.1002/cfp2.1010.

Schwartz, B. (2004). The paradox of choice: Why more is less. New York: Ecco.

Sullivan, P. S., Lansky, A., & Drake, A. (2004). Failure to return for HIV test results among persons at high risk for HIV infection: Results from a multistate interview project. JAIDS Journal of Acquired Immune Deficiency Syndromes, 35(5), 511–518.

Thaler, R. H. (1990). Anomalies: Saving, fungibility, and mental accounts. The Journal of Economic Perspectives, 4, 193-205.

Thaler, R. H., & Johnson, E. J. (1990). Gambling with the house money and trying to break even: The effects of prior outcomes on risky choice. Management Science, 36(6), 643-660.

Thorndike, A. N., Sonnenberg, L., Riis, J., Barraclough, S., & Levy, D. E. (2012). A 2-phase labeling and choice architecture intervention to improve healthy food and beverage choices. American Journal of Public Health, 102(3), 527-533.

Tversky, A., & Kahneman, D. (1974). Judgment under uncertainty: Heuristics and biases. Science (New Series), 185, 1124-1131.

Zellermayer, O. (1996). The pain of paying. (Doctoral dissertation). Department of Social and Decision Sciences, Carnegie Mellon University, Pittsburgh, PA.

www.ingramcontent.com/pod-product-compliance
Ingram Content Group UK Ltd.
Pitfield, Milton Keynes, MK11 3LW, UK
UKHW041639190726
13854UKWH00006B/2594

9 798885 913874